Bold Women
in
Nevada History

KAY
MOORE

BOLD WOMEN IN NEVADA HISTORY

KAY MOORE

2019
Mountain Press Publishing Company
Missoula, Montana

Cover art © 2019 Stephanie Frostad (stephaniefrostad.com);
photographed by Christofer Autio (chrisautio.com)

Map on page iv by Chelsea Feeney (cmcfeeney.com)

Library of Congress Cataloging-in-Publication Data

Names: Moore, Kay, 1950- author.
Title: Bold women in Nevada history / Kay Moore.
Description: Missoula, Montana : Mountain Press Publishing Company, 2019. |
  Series: Bold women series | Includes bibliographical references and index.
Identifiers: LCCN 2019013962 | ISBN 9780878426959 (pbk. : alk. paper)
Subjects: LCSH: Women—Nevada—Biography. | Women—Nevada—History. |
  Nevada—Biography.
Classification: LCC CT3262.N38 M66 2019 | DDC 920.7209793—dc23
LC record available at https://lccn.loc.gov/2019013962

PRINTED IN THE UNITED STATES

MP Mountain Press
PUBLISHING COMPANY
P.O. Box 2399 • Missoula, MT 59806 • 406-728-1900
800-234-5308 • info@mtnpress.com
www.mountain-press.com

*To the members of the Nevada Women's History Project
and the Southern Nevada Women's History Project,
whose ongoing efforts promote the various and important
roles women played in state history*

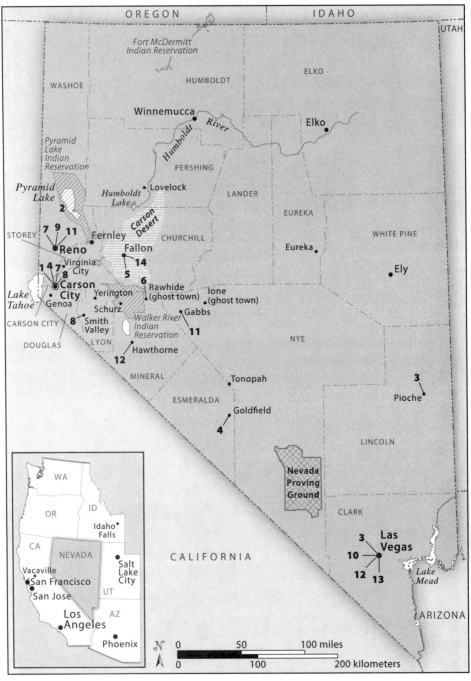

OREGON   IDAHO

UTAH

Fort McDermitt Indian Reservation

WASHOE

HUMBOLDT

ELKO

Winnemucca

Elko

Pyramid Lake Indian Reservation

PERSHING

Pyramid Lake

Humboldt River

Lovelock

LANDER

Humboldt Lake

EUREKA

WHITE PINE

7   9   11
STOREY

Fernley

Carson Desert

2

CHURCHILL

Eureka

Reno

Fallon

Ely

1 4 7
8
Virginia
City

14

5

6

Rawhide
(ghost town)

Ione
(ghost town)

**Carson
City**

Yerington

NYE

*Lake
Tahoe*

Genoa

Schurz

Gabbs

CARSON CITY

8   Smith
Valley

*Walker River
Indian
Reservation*

11

DOUGLAS

LYON

12   Hawthorne

MINERAL

3

Tonopah

Pioche

ESMERALDA

Goldfield

4

LINCOLN

**Nevada
Proving
Ground**

CLARK

WA

ID

OR

*Idaho
Falls*

NEVADA

CA

3   **Las
Vegas**

10

Vacaville

*Salt
Lake
City*

12   13

*Lake
Mead*

San Francisco

San Jose

UT

CALIFORNIA

ARIZONA

Los
Angeles

AZ

Phoenix

N

0   50   100 miles

0   100   200 kilometers

1. Hannah Keziah Clapp
2. Sarah Winnemucca Hopkins
3. Helen Jane Wiser Stewart
4. Felice Cohn
5. Wuzzie Dick George
6. Anna Frances Elleser Rechel
7. Thérèse Alpetche Laxalt

8. Mary Hill Fulstone
9. Alice Lucretia Smith and Bertha Woodard
10. Lilly Ong Hing Fong
11. Velma Bronn Johnston
12. Sarann Knight Preddy
13. Geneva Ann Smith Douglas
14. Marcia de Braga

CONTENTS

ACKNOWLEDGMENTS

The goal of a nonfiction writer is to track down accurate, interesting information. While research in books and documents can provide this, it often takes the knowledge and expertise of others to interpret the data found or provide answers to the quirky questions that bother authors. My deepest gratitude to the following people who responded to my inquiries for information and photographs:

Bobbi Ohlinger, Attorney; John Ekman, President of the Goldfield Historical Society; Soroptimist International of Fallon; Doris Dowden, Communications, American Association of University Women, Nevada; Bunny Corkill, whose memories of her friend Marcia de Braga made me laugh and cry; Churchill County Museum; Barbara Hodges, Photograph Curator, Churchill County Museum & Archives, Fallon; Natalie Luvera, Curator, National Atomic Testing Museum, Las Vegas; David C. Bugli, Secretary, Carson City Historical Society, Carson City; Terry Rubenstein, Regent, Nevada State Society Daughters of the American Revolution; Kathy Lowe, Silver State Chapter, Daughters of the American Revolution, Boulder City; Dr. Linda Miller, Las Vegas; Beth Hewitt, Park Supervisor, Old Las Vegas Mormon Fort State Historic Park; Allison St. Germain, Director of Technology, Delta Zeta Sorority, Oxford, Ohio; Sheryln L. Hayes-Zorn, Curator of Manuscripts, Nevada Historical Society; Teresa Wilt, Legislative Librarian, Research Library, Legislative Counsel Bureau; Susan Furlong, Chief Clerk of the Assembly, Carson City; Patti Bernard, Chair, Nevada Women's History Project; Mary Gafford, Southern Nevada Women's History Project; Pat Casey; Frank Estrella, Ghost Town Explorer; Heidi Bunch, *Mineral County Independent-News*; Kimberly Roberts, Photograph Curator, Special Collections Department, University of Nevada, Reno; Sean Busey, Special Collections & University Archives, University of Nevada, Reno; and Delores Brownlee, Library Tech IV, University of Nevada Las Vegas. Special thanks to Jennifer Carey, my wonderful editor at Mountain Press who, aided by Megan McInerney, caught my errors and added clarity to my thoughts. Stephanie Frostad's art and Chelsea Feeney's map add strong visual appeal to my book. I was honored to have Mark Hall-Patton, who took time from his busy schedule as a curator of multiple museums in the Las Vegas area and historical consultant on the television show "Pawn Stars," to read and respond to my manuscript. As always, the support of my son Bryan and his family means the world to me as I continue my quest to help readers hear the lost voices of the past and appreciate the contributions these people made that greatly enriched our world.

INTRODUCTION

HOME MEANS NEVADA

Home means Nevada, Home *means the hills,*
Home *means the sage and the pines.*
Out by the Truckee's silvery rills,
Out where the sun always shines.
There is the land that I love the best,
Fairer than all I can see,
Right in the heart of the golden west
Home *means Nevada to me.*

—BERTHA RAFFETTO

Although Nevada is commonly perceived as a vast, poorly inhabited state—except for the areas around the cities of Las Vegas and Reno—the chorus of Bertha Raffetto's state song, "Home Means Nevada," outlines the true geographic diversity of the region. Nevada is among the most mountainous states in the Lower 48 and sometimes snow is present on peaks year round. The name *Nevada* is Spanish for "snow-capped." There are more than 150 named mountain ranges, and the highest point in the state is Boundary Peak at 13,140 feet in the White Mountains.

Despite—and even because of—the mountains, the state is arid. Nevada receives the least amount of rain in the United States, with only about nine and a half inches each year. The imposing Sierra Nevada along the California–Nevada border creates a rain shadow, limiting precipitation. The Great Basin Desert occupies the northern part of the state, and the Mojave Desert stretches across the south. Although Nevada ranks as the seventh-largest state, around 85 percent of that land is federally owned. Nevadans tend to be fiercely protective of their land holdings because private ownership is so limited.

Nevada's official nickname, the Silver State, touts the metal that first drew permanent settlers to the territory. Many miners passed through Nevada on their way to California after the 1848 discovery of gold at Sutter's Mill. Ten years later, the Comstock Lode silver deposit brought some of the miners back and attracted many others to the area. Producing nearly $70 million of silver over the next eight years, Nevada sent much of this to Washington DC after it became a territory on March 2, 1861. The silver helped finance the Union effort to defeat the seceded southern states during the Civil War (1861–1865). Today, only Alaska surpasses Nevada in silver production.

Nevada obtained statehood during the Civil War, which is why the slogan "Battle Born" appears on the state flag. President Abraham Lincoln wanted an additional northern state that would support him in the 1864 presidential election. In order to make that happen in time for the November 7 election, the entire state constitution was sent by telegraph to the US Congress. The transmission took two days, from October 26 to 27; consisted of 16,543 words; and cost $4,303.27 to send—equivalent to over $65,000 in 2018. At the time, the telegraph set a record for the longest transmission ever sent. President Lincoln proclaimed Nevada the thirty-sixth state on October 31, 1864, and he won the election a week later.

Perhaps Nevada's creation during a turbulent time in America's past is also what imbued its citizens with a strong sense of independence. The boom-and-bust cycles created by mining acted as societal roller coasters that continually scattered people around the state and created the many ghost towns that still dot Nevada's landscape. In these early days, if a behavior wasn't specifically forbidden by law, the prevailing attitude was that it was acceptable in Nevada. Over the years, the state embraced what most of the rest of the country considered vices: prizefighting was permitted in 1897; gambling was legalized in March 1931; and divorce was an important industry in the state, with Reno being considered the divorce capital of the world for six decades (1900s to 1960s). All of these activities helped increase the population base and fostered economic stability by drawing many visitors to the state.

Nevada's liberal stance allowed women of various backgrounds to break out of the era's traditional gender roles. Despite being outnumbered by male residents for decades, they questioned the authority of men and entered male-dominated professions. Women braved the harsh, often lonely, living conditions and thrived by various means, although married women were usually "housekeepers" when census takers asked. It was due to women's actions that Nevada became a "home," as the state song suggests, not just land to travel through on the way to somewhere else.

Professor Hannah Keziah Clapp, circa 1900. —University Libraries, Special Collections Department [UNRA-P174-01], University of Nevada, Reno

HANNAH KEZIAH CLAPP
(1824–1908)

Education Was Her Game—
Versatility Made Her Fame

In June 1876, Hannah trembled with excitement at the thought of attending the Centennial Exhibition in Philadelphia, Pennsylvania— the first major World's Fair to be held in the United States. Its official name was the International Exhibition of Arts, Manufactures and Products of the Soil and Mine. Traveling across the country by train from Carson City with fellow teacher Elizabeth "Eliza" Cilicia Babcock, Hannah became one of the nearly ten million visitors. Only forty-six million people inhabited the whole country at the time, so almost one-fifth of the population attended the fair. Paying their fifty-cent admission fees, the two women marveled at the exhibits from thirty-seven nations in more than 250 buildings. The goal of the event was to showcase the United States as a rising industrial world power. Philadelphia, with its many cultural and industrial venues, was selected as the host city because the celebration also commemorated the 100th anniversary of the signing of the Declaration of Independence.

The two women made quite a unique pair walking around the fairgrounds. Hannah wore bloomer dresses (short dresses with pants) or dark suits and solid, flat-heeled shoes. A gold watch rested in one pocket of her skirt with its chain crossing her body to settle in another pocket. Her deep voice and brusque manner commanded attention. The sun highlighted her pink cheeks, clear blue eyes, and very short curly hair, which was unusual for that time. In contrast, Eliza was small and slender, dainty in her traditional dress, and displayed a gentle manner.

Hannah and Eliza were both teachers, so they must have enjoyed seeing the book-making exhibit. The entire process, from milling the paper to printing the book, was on display in the Campbell Printing Press Building. The final product was a book called *Something for the Children* and provided young readers an overview of the Centennial Exhibition of 1876.

The display of mining equipment at Machinery Hall probably reminded them of home because Carson City was a supply point for many mining operations. Like others, Hannah and Eliza marveled at all the new products being introduced to the public for the first time: typewriters, a mechanical calculator, Alexander Graham Bell's telephone, and Thomas Edison's automatic telegraph, which allowed faster transmissions than earlier machines. They may have tasted a new food product called Heinz Tomato Ketchup and enjoyed a free glass of Hires Root Beer. Hannah and Eliza must also have appreciated the Women's Pavilion, where everything was by or for women—the first time women received major recognition at such an event. Hannah bought a hand-painted china punch bowl and a silver ladle as souvenirs.

But Hannah and Eliza had come to the World's Fair specifically to see one exhibit: the Kindergarten Cottage, an annex to the Women's Pavilion. Classes were conducted with young children in front of large audiences each day. The teacher used methods drawn from the work of the innovative German educator Friedrich Froebel, which included educational play materials, such as blocks with patterns, for the children to identify and group. Other blocks were shaped in various sizes for building structures. Games and songs were also included in the curriculum. These techniques were very different from the memorization and oral recitation commonly used by American teachers. Froebel created the term *kindergarten* ("child garden" in his native German), demonstrating his belief that learning should be enjoyable.

Hannah and Eliza returned home to Nevada in October, determined to start a kindergarten. Prior to 1870, there were only ten kindergartens in the whole United States and none in Nevada. In 1877, Hannah opened a program for six-year-olds in the basement of the school she had founded in Carson City. This progressive project was one of many Hannah accomplished in her lifetime, in education as well as in other fields.

———•••———

Information about Hannah's childhood is scarce and even her date of birth is unclear. Her gravestone states that she was born on July 5, 1827, but other records indicate that her birth occurred in March 1824. The earlier date seems to be more accurate based on when she started teaching and makes her the fourth-oldest of eight children born to parents Horatio Orris and Hannah Bangs Clapp in Saratoga, New York. Her sister Elethea and brothers Israel and William were older, while Lucy, Sarah Jane, Allen, and Nathan were younger. Her father, born in New York, was a Presbyterian minister, and her mother was from Charleston, South Carolina. Hannah may have inherited her "fearless and extraordinarily energetic" nature, as described by Dante Pistone in his article "Carson City Heroine," from her maternal grandfather, Reverend Michael Burdge, who reportedly threw tea into Boston Harbor in 1773 and later served bravely in the continental troops from New York.

The earliest historical record of Hannah shows that she began her career as an educator at age twenty-five at Union Seminary in Ypsilanti, Michigan, where she taught from 1849 to 1854. She was then appointed principal of one of Michigan's first colleges, the Female Seminary, which opened in Lansing in September 1855. She later taught at the Michigan Female College in Kalamazoo and was one of the founding members of that faculty.

In 1859, Hannah boldly decided to leave her stable job and venture west, traveling via wagon train with her brother Nathan and his family. Somewhere along the way, in her calico blouse and bloomers, Hannah caught the eye of an Indian chief who offered to trade some ponies in exchange for her. The offer was declined, but the incident tickled Hannah, who loved to tell this story later in life.

Arriving first in Salt Lake City, Utah, Hannah had the opportunity to meet Brigham Young, the leader of the Church of Jesus Christ of Latter-day Saints (known as Mormons) during her weeklong stay. It is said that she attended Mormon services wearing a bloomer dress and a hat with a revolver slung on her hip. A devout feminist—even before the word garnered its meaning of advocating for women's rights—Hannah was upset with how the Mormon women were treated, noting in a letter to a friend back in Lansing that they were "miserable slaves." She also felt like she was in a foreign country because the Mormon flag was more prevalent than the American flag.

Joining the wagon train of the Perkins family, Hannah continued on to California, settling in Vacaville, south of Sacramento. She taught at a school there until the fall of 1860, when the Perkins family, who was heading to Nevada, asked her to accompany them again. Hannah arrived in Carson City, the little town named for frontiersman and scout Kit Carson, on September 12, 1860. She noted the lack of schools in the "Washoe" area (the region east of the Sierra Nevada) and worked with another resident, Ellen Cutler, to organize a private coeducational school.

Supported by the territorial legislature, Governor James Warren Nye signed the bill of approval for the school on November 14, 1861. It probably helped that Hannah and Margaret Ormsby (widow of Major William Ormsby, a founder of Carson City, who was killed at the first battle of the Pyramid Lake War) donated cloth-covered "comfortable seats" to the legislature when it met for its first session in an old barn in October of that year. Sierra Seminary, as the school was officially called, became the first legally chartered school in Nevada. Attitudes about children and teaching techniques were changing, and Hannah wanted to be in the forefront of educational reform. Her vision shaped the path of education in Nevada.

Constructed at the corner of West Telegraph and North Minnesota Streets, the Sierra Seminary was very successful by the end of 1864 and was often called "Miss Clapp's School." Mark Twain, in his role as a reporter for the *Territorial Enterprise*, visited the school in December 1864 and again the following month. After his January visit, Twain noted: "The present school is a credit both to the teachers and the town. It now numbers forty students, I should think, and is well and systematically conducted." Twain later incorporated his observations of Hannah's teaching methods and final examinations (although his teacher is a man) in his book *Tom Sawyer* (1876):

> At eight in the evening . . . . The master sat throned in his great chair upon a raised platform . . . . Three rows of benches on each side and six rows in front of him were occupied by the dignitaries of the town and by the parents of the pupils. To his left . . . were seated the scholars . . . ; rows of small boys, washed and dressed to an intolerable state of discomfort; rows of gawky big boys; snowbanks of girls and young ladies clad in lawn and muslin . . . . The exercises began . . . . The prime feature of the evening was . . . original "compositions" by the young ladies.
>
> —Chapter XXI ("Examination Evening")

Mrs. Cutler had left Carson City in the spring of 1864, so the school needed to hire another teacher. Advertisements for a teacher of English and Latin were placed in newspapers in California. One respondent was a young woman from Orono, Maine, who happened to be visiting relatives in Stockton, California. After a series of letters, Eliza Babcock was hired as an assistant principal. Together, the two women made the Sierra Seminary one of the best schools in Nevada, with space for forty boarding pupils as well as day students. Many of these students went on to gain local and national prominence, including George Washington Gale Ferris Jr., who invented the Ferris Wheel that was displayed at the 1893 Chicago World's Fair.

Hannah avidly supported the temperance movement, an attempt to decrease the overconsumption of alcohol and promote abstinence. One day, she saw a drunken man come out of the Ormsby House, a saloon at the corner of Second and Carson Streets, and fall into the gutter. Respectable women did not enter saloons, so she went to the saloon door, knocked, and waited until the proprietor came out. Pointing at the prone man, she told the owner, "Your sign has fallen down. You'd better prop it up."

In the 1870s, the Chinese in Nevada were often targeted by other residents and endured much prejudice and discrimination. Hannah did not support this attitude. The issue of the *Carson Daily Appeal* on February 18, 1870, reported: "Miss H. K. Clapp has a class of some 30 Chinamen who attend a night school at the Sierra Seminary each evening in the week." The article also noted that Hannah received no payment for this effort.

But Hannah used her solid business sense to make the school profitable. She also speculated on mining stocks, including mines run by the Belcher Silver Mine Company, and became a wealthy woman (as did Eliza, who also invested). This income supported Hannah and Eliza's trip to Philadelphia in 1876 and provided funds for a house they had built on the northwest edge of the city. The *Carson Daily Appeal* noted in 1873 that a hired gardener cared for the landscaping around the "Clapp-Babcock place." Their combined personal worth may have been as high as $100,000.

Another profitable endeavor came in 1875 when legislation was passed to incorporate Carson City. The Capitol Grounds Improvement Act provided $23,000 for the repair of the State House and enclosure of the land in front of the building. The citizens were tired of the muddy field caused by cows and other animals that gathered there. Imagine the surprise of the other bidders (all men) when H. K. Clapp, the name Hannah used on her bid, was awarded the contract to supply the fencing material, undercutting the other bids by $350. The *Carson Daily Appeal* stated: "Let there be no further complaints about the nonenjoyment of their rights by the women of Nevada. The contract for furnishing the iron fencing for the Capitol Square has been awarded to the Misses Clapp and Babcock, Principals of Sierra Seminary; their bid $5,550 in coin for the delivery of the fencing upon the grounds is the lowest by some hundreds of dollars of those submitted."

The wrought iron was ordered from Philadelphia. It was preconstructed according to Hannah's specifications in ten-to-twelve-foot sections and then shipped by rail to Carson City. The first load arrived on July 30, 1875. By August 7, the entire amount was ready

Fence at the Nevada state capitol on Carson Street in Carson City. —Library of Congress

to be installed. A contractor and his work crew from the state prison fashioned a footing of sandstone blocks, mined from the quarry at the prison, and drilled holes in the sandstone for the iron posts, which were set in place with molten sulphur. On September 1, 1875, the fence was complete and had been given a coat of brown paint. The women made $1,000 in profit, and the construction was so solid that the fence still exists today, although some restoration was begun in 2016. Mining investments started slumping in 1880 and wiped out some of Hannah's assets, so she worked for the Nevada State Assembly as a committee clerk in 1883 and was later hired as a copying clerk for the state senate in the 1885 legislative session.

If women could handle men's work, it made no sense to Hannah that they couldn't vote or hold office. Often receiving advice from William M. Stewart, who had served as a US Senator for Nevada (1864–1875), she supported the equal franchise resolutions that the Nevada legislature considered in 1883, 1885, 1887, and 1889. These efforts to allow women the right to vote were rejected, but Hannah, undeterred, continued her political activism and in 1895, she was elected vice president of the Nevada Equal Suffrage Association in Reno. Although women in the United States did not achieve the right to vote until the ratification of the Nineteenth Amendment in 1920, Hannah's work still had a big influence on other Nevada women such as Annie Martin, who became the editor of the *Carson News* and provided coverage of women's issues in its articles.

The Civil War (1861–1865) was still prominent in the minds of citizens in 1884. Hannah became the first president of the Custer Women's Relief Corps No. 15, which was created in Carson City with twenty charter members. It was an auxiliary of the Grand Army of the Republic, a fraternal organization formed by veterans from the Union forces. The group's purpose was to assist veterans of the Civil War. Members promoted patriotic education and advocated for the establishment of regular pensions for veterans. Always a history buff, Hannah also became a charter member of the Nevada

Historical Society in 1904. Her travels throughout the state provided many artifacts for the new organization.

After high school, students had to leave the state to continue their education. Finally, in 1874, a framework for the creation of Nevada's first state university was included in the Nevada State Constitution. Originally organized in Elko, the Nevada State Legislature approved moving the campus to Reno in 1885. President Leroy Brown hired Hannah as the University of Nevada's first faculty member. She taught history and English and also acted as a campus librarian and a counselor for the female students.

The first building on the campus, Morrill Hall, was named for the congressional act that had provided money for the establishment of colleges that taught agricultural and mechanical arts as well as a traditional curriculum. In 1886, when classes started, there was no electricity or gas to light Morrill Hall. Hannah later noted that they literally "burned the midnight oil" to make the rooms useable. She recalled: "When I think of the fine scholarly work that was done in those early days of the institution . . . it seems it could have been nothing short of a special direction . . . . The Sierras shut us in on the Pacific side, and a very weary stretch of almost uninhabited plains separated us from the Atlantic Coast." The university library became Hannah's main assignment toward the end of her time on campus. When she retired in 1901 at age seventy-seven, with the distinguished title of professor emeritus, the library, thanks to her efforts, had expanded into multiple rooms that housed six thousand books and five thousand pamphlets.

While in Reno, Hannah became a founding member of the Twentieth Century Club, a national progressive women's group started in 1894. Its motto was: "The measure of the worth of an organization to its community, is bound in its ability to embrace opportunities for service." The Reno group funded a scholarship to the University of Nevada in 1898. Hannah was also instrumental in getting the club to organize the Reno Kindergarten Association and worked with members of the legislature to establish public kindergartens throughout Nevada. Club members also participated in tree-planting programs and worked to ban spitting on the city streets. This organization still exists and is considered the oldest active women's club in the state. They no longer meet at the original site, which was built on First Street in 1925, but the building was placed on the National Register of Historic Places on April 21, 1983.

A stroke in August 1896 left Eliza very ill and slightly paralyzed. Hannah took her to San Francisco for medical care, but Eliza never fully recovered and she died on September 19, 1899. In her honor, Hannah offered $1,000 to build the Elizabeth Babcock Memorial Kindergarten in Reno, and another $4,000 was raised via donations. The school was constructed on Sixth and West Avenues and completed in December 1901.

Following Froebel's ideas of a "child garden," the classroom walls were decorated with flowing vines, flittering butterflies, and soaring birds. The Reno Kindergarten Association ran the kindergarten until 1932, when the Reno School District bought the building. The old schoolhouse was used for various purposes until March 1966, when it was razed. During deconstruction, the cornerstone, which was laid in May 1901, was found with a tin box containing period newspapers; photos of the school's founders; a poem by Kate Tupper Galpin, who held a professorship of pedagogy (teaching) at the University; bylaws of the Reno Kindergarten Association; and a list of the people who donated for its construction.

Hannah felt Eliza's loss deeply, and in 1901 she decided to move to Palo Alto, California, where the two had purchased land in 1890 and where William Danforth Bliss, a well-known architect and former student of Hannah's, had designed and completed a Queen Anne-style house for the pair in 1896. After a three-month illness caused by heart problems, Hannah passed away there on October 8, 1908, at the age of eighty-four. The *Reno Evening Gazette* included in her obituary a resolution passed by the Kindergarten Association upon news of her death. It read, in part: "It is doubtful if any single individual has had a wider influence in the forming days of Nevada than Miss Clapp. In her case the reverse will be seen of the adage: The evil that men do lives after them: the good is interred with their bones. The good effects of Miss Clapp's life will be felt for generations to come, and if she had faults, they are all forgotten."

The University of Nevada held a memorial service for her eight days later. The Secretary of the Nevada Historical Society noted: "Other women have left their mark on one little community of our Commonwealth, but this one only is borne in the hearts of people north, south, east and west. . . . So ought the portrait of Hannah K. Clapp to be placed besides the oil paintings of our Governors in the Capitol; it should hang on the walls of this University, as well as the Kindergarten in Reno, and it should and shall be placed in the portrait gallery of the Nevada Historical Society, of which she was a charter member."

Hannah is buried at Mount Hope Cemetery in Bangor, Maine, in the plot of the Babcock family. Her Palo Alto house served as a community resource for women called Deborah's Palm from 2009–2018. According to their website, it was a "place for women to gather, receive encouragement, support and information." Hannah would have found this a fitting tribute for her.

Hannah's humanitarian efforts—especially to help children—have been honored by the Committee to Aid Abused Women. Begun in 1982, the Hannah Humanitarian Award is presented annually at a fundraising luncheon that helps raise money to support the group's work. The honor is bestowed upon a Nevadan who has actively worked to create a more caring environment in the state. Also, in recognition of her strong speaking skills, the Nevada Women's History Project instituted the Hannah Clapp Lecture Series, which offers informative programs about women from Nevada's past. Hannah Clapp Street, located in southern Las Vegas, is also named for her.

Found among Hannah's papers after her death was the following quote, which she had copied: "People who do nothing as a rule, know nothing, and never have time to be of use to anybody, not even themselves." Perhaps this quote motivated her to challenge the expectations for women in her era and dedicate her life to education. Her feisty and assertive personality must have contributed to the many times she butted heads with men and fought so hard for women's suffrage. However, her deep and ongoing concern for the young demonstrated a softer core. Perhaps that is why she donated the bell from the Sierra Seminary, which she used to ring in order to call recess, to the Nevada State Museum. It symbolized how she wanted to be remembered—as a champion for children.

2

SARAH WINNEMUCCA HOPKINS
(1844–1891)

The Voice of the Paiutes

Patrons of Platt's Hall on Montgomery Street in San Francisco, California, tittered with excitement. Although political rallies and sporting events were held here, usually the wealthy and well-to-do citizens of the city enjoyed music or a theatrical performance as they relaxed on the luxurious cushioned seats. But on this November night in 1879, they were going to hear a presentation by a princess. For weeks, notices had been posted around the city advertising the speaker: Sarah Winnemucca, "the Piute Princess." Since the majority of the city dwellers knew little of the indigenous population, only the small print phrase "Indian maiden" may have given them a clue that the speaker was not a visiting royal.

For the audience that night, Sarah Winnemucca might as well have come from a foreign land. Most of what they knew about the indigenous population came from newspaper articles, so they didn't understand that the culture did not include the concept of royalty. Sarah was the daughter of a chief, but describing her as a "princess" was for promotional purposes, not accuracy. Sarah's tribe was referred to then as the Piute, Pi-Utah, or Pah-Ute, but today is known as the Paiute.

The nineteenth-century press usually described all native people as savage and aggressive. Consequently, the audience members who

Studio portrait of Sarah Winnemucca Hopkins in beaded dress and moccasins, circa 1883. —Photo by Elmer Chickering

knew Sarah's background were expecting her to appear in war paint and crude attire. Imagine their shock when Sarah demurely walked on stage wearing, as one reporter described, "a short, buckskin dress, the skirt bordered with fringe and embroidery, short sleeves, disclosing beautifully rounded brown arms and scarlet leggins, with trimmings of fringe. On her head she wore a proud head dress of eagle's feathers, set in a scarlet crown, contrasting well with her flowing black locks."

Sarah surprised them again when she spoke easily in English about the history and poor condition of her people, whom she referred to as the "Numa," using stories, gestures, and humor to make her points. Her presentation was such a success that she was invited to repeat the event on several dates in December. One local newspaper, the *Daily Evening Bulletin*, reported: "Last night, Sarah Winnemucca, daughter of the Chief of the Piutes, repeated her lecture . . . before a very good audience at Platt's Hall. . . . Sarah's efforts on the rostrum have made such a favorable impression on her friends that they have persuaded her to repeat her lecture next Saturday and Monday evenings at Platt's Hall."

To showcase more of her tribe and garner public support for her people, Sarah sometimes had her brother Natchez give a short talk, which she translated, and had a few other men sing a Paiute chant. But Sarah was the one people wanted to see, and they reacted to her with cheers and applause, even when her words were critical: "The proverb says the big fish eat the little fishes, and we Indians are the little fish and you eat us all up and drive us from home. Where can we poor Indians go if the government will not help us? If your people will help us, and you have good hearts, . . . I will promise to educate my people and make them law-abiding citizens of the United States. It can be done—it can be done."

The *San Francisco Chronicle* further outlined what Sarah hoped to accomplish: "Her mission, undertaken at the request of Chief Winnemucca, is to have her tribe gathered together again at their old home in Nevada, where they can follow peaceable pursuits and improve themselves." Although Sarah's efforts in San Francisco did not raise much money for her people, it did garner her publicity prior to a trip east, which included a meeting with the President of the United States at the White House in Washington DC—quite an accomplishment for an indigenous woman who was once a little girl afraid that white men would eat her.

———•••———

Originally named Thocmetony (Shell Flower), Sarah was born in 1844 near Humboldt Lake in what was then Utah Territory. Like most girls in her tribe, she was named for a flower. Born in the pine nut season, which would have been September or October, Sarah was the daughter of Chief Winnemucca and Tuboitonie (sometimes spelled Tuboitony), the daughter of Chief Truckee. Sarah had three older brothers (Tom, Natchez, and Lee) and an older sister, Mary. Her mother had another daughter (Elma) before being killed in 1865 during a US Calvary raid on the tribe. Sarah's grandfather was the chief of the entire Northern Paiute nation and had assisted General John C. Frémont in the Bear Flag Rebellion (1846) when Americans rebelled against Mexico for the control of California.

The Northern Paiutes were normally peaceful people who lived in bands throughout present-day northwestern Nevada, northeastern California, and southeastern Oregon. They hunted and gathered their food, so they changed locales as needed, but considered the land around Pyramid Lake in Nevada to be their home. Sarah's father acted as band chief of the Kuyuidika when Chief Truckee was working as a guide for the soldiers. When he returned, Chief Truckee regaled the children with stories of how the white men lived. They were amazed to hear of buildings three stories high and a "big house that runs on the river, and it whistles and makes a beautiful noise."

While steamboats were impressive, it was writing that got Chief Truckee to trust his "white brothers." They gave him a letter, which stated that Chief Truckee had helped the United States defeat Mexico. He called the piece of paper his "rag friend." Because the Paiutes had no written language, the idea of scribbles on tattered paper having meaning seemed magical to most of them. Chief Winnemucca, however, was leery of these white men and tried to distance himself and his band of people from them as much as possible.

As a child, Sarah watched from afar as the "houses on wheels" traveled slowly across the desert. She later recounted that mothers had told their children "that the whites were killing everybody and eating them." Her own mother once buried Sarah in sand up to her head, which she covered with sagebrush in order to save Sarah from the perceived threat of white immigrants. Imagine the terror felt by a child who spent a whole day in this manner until her mother dug her up again at night. With light, round eyes and hair on their faces, Sarah equated white men to "Cannibal Owl" from an old tribal legend about a bird that captured misbehaving children, beat them into a pulp, and ate them.

Sarah found herself caught between the two opinions. She loved her grandfather immensely, so ultimately she decided that the white men must have some good or he wouldn't admire them. She was somewhat excited when her grandfather decided to move his band to California to learn the lifestyle of the white immigrants in 1851. Chief Winnemucca refused to go, as did most of the rest of the band. However, Chief Truckee insisted his daughter and her children— including six-year-old Sarah—had to go.

After traveling for several days, the group stopped at a ranch near the San Joaquin River (near present-day Stockton). The men were hired as ranch hands, and the women worked in the house. Sarah slept in a bed for the first time. Initially, she was afraid of new things such as soft, fabric-covered chairs and colorful dishes filled with strange food, but she grew to like these new luxuries. Around this time, the ranchers began to call her "Sarah" because they felt her tribal name was too hard to pronounce. After seven years, the native people tired of the white lifestyle and decided to return to the others. This experience allowed Sarah to better understand her father's point of view.

When the group returned to present-day northern Nevada, life was much more difficult. It had never been easy for the Paiutes to survive in the harsh desert region. They usually greeted each other by saying *"uduta hada,"* which means "it's hot." Now, with more people settling around them, they had to go into the mountains to find food.

In 1857, perhaps because of food scarcities, Chief Truckee arranged for Sarah and her sister Elma to work for Major William Ormsby at Mormon Station (now Genoa, Nevada). They would help with household chores and serve customers in the store and stagecoach stop that he owned. When Mrs. Ormsby taught her daughter Lizzie to read and write, Sarah learned too. Within a year, she was fairly fluent in English, adding it to the languages she already knew—three Indian dialects (Paiute, Washoe, and Shoshone) and Spanish.

Chief Truckee became very ill in 1860 from an infection on his hand, probably from an insect bite. Before he died, he asked one of his "white brothers" to take Sarah and Elma to the nuns at the Academy of Notre Dame in San Jose, California, which still exists as Notre Dame High School. He wanted the girls to continue their education. Sixteen-year-old Sarah loved being at the school. She especially enjoyed learning needlework. However, the mothers of the other students objected to the presence of the Paiute girls, and the nuns were forced to return the girls to their tribe after only a few weeks.

Conditions continued to spiral downward for Sarah's people. A vein of silver had been discovered in Paiute territory in 1859, and the tribe competed for land with the miners and other settlers who flocked to the area. Proponents of a transcontinental railroad were also eyeing Paiute land. President Abraham Lincoln appointed James Warren Nye as governor of the Nevada Territory on March 2, 1861, and he also served as superintendent of Indian Affairs. Although Sarah later stated that he was "the only governor who ever helped my people," she meant that in reference to protecting them from white settlers. The Paiute tribe did receive some material things such as clothing and food, but the desire of the federal government was to move all of the native people onto a reservation.

Chief Winnemucca, the tribal leader after Chief Truckee's death in 1860, stayed at Pyramid Lake in northwestern Nevada on land set aside by the government in 1859 for a reservation. The Walker River Indian Reservation in central Nevada was established at the same time, both being formally recognized in 1874 by President Ulysses S. Grant. Sarah traveled from one reservation to another, trying to help her people. During this time frame, Sarah, Elma, their father, and some other Paiute men began performing at a theater. Billed as the "Paiute Royal Family," they passed a hat around afterwards to collect much-needed donations.

By 1868, the situation was desperate. Sarah went to Camp McDermit near the Oregon border to request army assistance. Her language ability was noted, and she was hired as an interpreter. Her brother brought about five hundred Paiutes to that camp for the winter. They chose relocation over starvation.

Sarah met New York–born First Lieutenant Edward C. Bartlett at Camp McDermit. She was enchanted by his carefree manner and expert horsemanship. He must have liked what he saw in her too. In February 1872, the *Nevada State Journal* described Sarah as "graceful in all her movements. Her jet black hair hangs in heavy curls, and her sparkling black eyes forbid anything tending to too much familiarity. She dresses very tastefully, but not extravagantly—a la Americaine, upon this occasion, in a tight fitting suit of black alpaca, very prettily trimmed with green fringe—in all making a very attractive appearance." Although interracial marriage was forbidden in Nevada, the two went to Salt Lake City, Utah, where a justice of the peace married them on January 29, 1872. Sarah quickly learned that Bartlett was a heavy drinker, and that he had pawned her few possessions to acquire money to buy liquor. The marriage only lasted one year, but according to the decree in the Grant County Courthouse in Canyon City, Oregon, it was not legally dissolved until September 21, 1876. She paid $69.62 in court fees to legally regain the name Sarah Winnemucca.

In 1870, desperate to help her people Sarah remembered how her grandfather had appreciated the power of the written word and she started a writing campaign. One letter, addressed to Ely Samuel Parker, the Commissioner of Indian Affairs, outlined the issues her tribe faced. It was later reprinted in several newspapers, *Harper's Magazine*, and the book *A Century of Dishonor* (1881) by Helen Hunt Jackson, who wrote fiction and nonfiction seeking justice for the mistreatment of tribes. In a newspaper article published in the *Californian* in September 1882, Sarah predicted: "I see very well that all of my race will die out. In a few short years there will be none left—no, not one Indian in the whole of America."

Life for the Paiutes kept changing depending on who acted as the agent for the reservations. When it was evident that her people were again desperate for the basic essentials of food and clothing, Sarah resolved to travel to Washington DC to meet with higher-level government officials. Her plan, however, was interrupted by the Bannock War.

In the spring of 1878, the Bannocks (whose tribal name comes from the Paiute word for "riverside") and some Paiutes chose to fight for their rights. Chief Winnemucca, who had traveled to the Bannock camp (near the Oregon–Idaho border) hoping to maintain peace, refused to ally with the Bannocks in war, so the Bannocks took him and his companions as prisoners. Acting under the authority of General Oliver Otis Howard, Sarah traveled with her brother Lee and his wife, Mattie, almost nonstop for three days into Idaho—about 220 miles on horseback—to rescue the hostages. Sneaking into the camp where the hostages were being held, the trio of rescuers helped seventy-five people escape. For the rest of the war, Sarah worked as an interpreter and scout for the military. The fighting finally ended in September 1878. Sarah was viewed as a tribal chief at this point due to her efforts to keep her people safe.

However, their good fortune did not last long. The Paiutes thought they would be able to stay at the Malheur Reservation in Oregon, where they had been living during the war. They were mistaken. The army ordered that all 540 members of the tribe be moved to the Yakima Reservation in Washington Territory. *Malheur* is the French word for "misfortune," perhaps an omen of things to come. Unprovisioned for a winter journey, the elderly, women, and babies died and were left unburied during the twenty-five-day trip in January 1879. This is sometimes known as the Paiute Trail of Tears. The agent in Washington had not been told they were coming, so no shelter, food, or clothing was available for them when they arrived.

Sarah's people again asked her to appeal on their behalf to the "Great White Father" in Washington DC, so she rekindled her plans to head east. Traveling through San Francisco, she performed at Platt's Hall. Upon her arrival in Washington DC, she met with Secretary of the Interior Carl Schurz, who promised the assistance of one hundred tents and food, and she crossed paths with President Rutherford B. Hayes in a waiting room. He asked, "Did you get all you wanted for your people?" Relying on Schurz's promise, she answered in the affirmative. However, she was unable to lecture or get media coverage of the plight of her tribe because officials kept her busy sightseeing. They had received a letter from the agent of the Malheur Reservation who made untrue claims about Sarah, and this undermined her credibility with the government.

Little did Sarah know that Schurz would break his word. She was blamed by her people, who believed she had betrayed them. Perhaps Sarah's feelings of isolation explain why she was drawn to Lewis H. Hopkins—a former Army soldier born in Tennessee and five years her junior—even though she had not had much luck with marriage (she had married and divorced two more times after Bartlett). Lewis and Sarah wed on December 5, 1881, in San Francisco. A California law prohibited marriage between races at this time, so they must have found a sympathetic clergyman. However, any record of the marriage or an exemption to the law would have been destroyed in the fires that broke out after the 1906 earthquake.

When Chief Winnemucca died in 1882, Natchez became chief. He asked Sarah to help the tribe again, and she agreed to another trip east. Arriving in Boston, she met Elizabeth Palmer Peabody and her sister, Mary Peabody Mann, the widow of well-known educator Horace Mann. Elizabeth and Sarah became friends. Elizabeth arranged for a lecture tour for her all over the East Coast from 1883 to 1884. Thousands of people in New York, Connecticut, Rhode Island, Maryland, Massachusetts, and Pennsylvania paid between ten and twenty-five cents to hear her presentations. Because Elizabeth was the first female book publisher in the United States, she also urged Sarah to record the history of her tribe. Written as an autobiography, *Life Among the Piutes: Their Wrongs and Claims* was published in 1883. The 268-page, leather-bound book, which sold for $1, is considered to be the first book written in English by an American Indian woman. Sarah was also the first of her race to receive a copyright.

Sarah met President Chester Arthur in the spring of 1884 but felt he really didn't listen to her pleas. She spoke before the US Congress on April 22, 1884, asking that the land around Pyramid Lake be given to her people. On July 6, 1884, a bill was passed that gave each family 160 acres of poor quality land around Malheur. However, it never happened, and Sarah chalked up the failure to another promise broken by the government. As she described it, "promises which, like the wind, were heard no more."

Sarah and her husband, Lewis, returned to Nevada and lived at Pyramid Lake. Railroad baron Leland Stanford became sympathetic to the Northern Paiute cause; he provided Sarah free passage on his railroads when she traveled. He also bought Sarah and her brother Natchez 160 acres near Lovelock (in today's Pershing County). Natchez farmed, and Sarah opened a school called Peabody's Institute, in honor of the Boston woman who helped finance the endeavor. Her rationale for opening a school was noted in an article in the *Winnemucca Silver State* on July 9, 1886: "It seems strange to me that the Government has not found out years ago that education is the key to the Indian problem. Much money and many precious lives would have been saved if the American people had fought my people with Books instead of Powder and lead. Education civilized your race and there is no reason why it cannot civilize mine." Her belief was also published that year in a pamphlet called "Sarah Winnemucca's Practical Solution to the Indian Problem." But keeping the school open was not easy because many disagreed with her philosophy that Indian children should be taught their native culture and language. Assimilation necessitated only speaking English. Conflicts with their neighbors arose.

Lewis died of consumption (now known as tuberculosis or TB) on October 26, 1887, as reported in the *Nevada State Journal*. He is supposedly buried in Lone Mountain Cemetery in Carson City. Sarah kept the school open until 1888. She then went to Henrys Lake (in present-day Idaho), to stay with her sister Elma. She observed: "When I think of my past life, and the bitter trials I have endured, I can scarcely believe I live, and yet I do; and, with the help of Him who notes the sparrow's fall, I mean to fight for my down-trodden race while life lasts."

Sarah died on October 17, 1891, probably also from TB. She was forty-seven years old. She is buried without a marker in what today is known as Targhee Cemetery in Fremont County, Idaho.

The *New York Times* printed an article about Sarah's passing and discussed important aspects of her life in the October 27, 1891, issue. The national recognition and fame of the little Paiute girl from Nevada continued into the twentieth century. General Oliver Otis

Howard, for whom Sarah had worked during the Bannock War, wrote a short biography of her in his 1908 book *Famous Indian Chiefs I Have Known*. He noted, "She did our government great service, and if I could tell you but a tenth part of all she willingly did to help the white settlers and her own people to live peaceably together I am sure you would think, as I do, that the name of Toc-me-to-ne (or Shell flower) should have a place beside the name of Pocahontas in the history of our country."

In 1993, Sarah was added to the Nevada Writers Hall of Fame for her book. In 1994, an elementary school in Reno (Washoe County School District) was named in her honor. She was the first woman to be given a Nevada state historic marker (no. 143). Located in Humboldt County, it is at the site of the Fort McDermitt Indian Reservation (no one knows when the extra "t" was added to the name because the original fort was named after Lt. Col. Charles McDermit, once a commander of the Military District of Nevada). Part of the inscription on the marker reads: "Here at Fort McDermitt as interpreter and teacher she served well both Indians and US military. This exceptional Indian woman, a leader of her race, believed in the brotherhood of mankind." In 1994, Sarah was inducted into the National Women's Hall of Fame in Seneca Falls, New York.

In 2001, Assemblywoman Marcia de Braga introduced a bill to the Nevada Legislature to make Sarah the subject of the second statue from Nevada to appear as part of the National Statuary Hall Collection in Washington DC. It passed unanimously. The sculpture, by Benjamin Victor, was unveiled on March 9, 2005. Sarah holds a shell flower (the source of her native name) and a copy of her book. The plaque at the bottom lists her accomplishments as follows: "Defender of Human Rights, Educator, and Author of First Book by a Native Woman." A duplicate statue can be seen in the Nevada State Capitol Building in Carson City. Sarah also continues to have ties to the field of education in various ways. Western Nevada

College's Sarah Winnemucca Hall, in the Aspen Building in Carson City, hosts musical as well as other types of programs.

While some relate the name of the Humboldt County city of Winnemucca, Nevada, to Sarah, it is really named for her father. The name *Winnemucca* has been translated as "one moccasin" or the "giver of spiritual gifts." However, either sentiment of caring aptly fits Sarah.

To help raise funds for the schools supported by the Daughters of the American Revolution (DAR), each year a different state agrees to furnish a doll for a raffle to benefit the scholarship fund established in 1938. The Nevada State Society of the DAR created the Sarah Winnemucca Junior Doll in 2016 for the drawing in 2021. Members and nonorganization members can purchase raffle tickets in hopes of winning the doll, which is styled and clothed to look like her namesake. Through this project, many people throughout the United States will learn the story of this courageous, persistent woman who became the voice of her people, and it is appropriate that Sarah Winnemucca receive this national recognition for her many accomplishments.

Helen J. Stewart in the late 1870s or 1880s. —Photo taken by Elite Photographic Studio in San Francisco; Helen J. Stewart Photo Collection [0104 007156]. UNLV Libraries Special Collections & Archives

3

HELEN JANE WISER STEWART
(1854–1926)

Pioneer First Lady of Las Vegas

A friend of Helen Jane Wiser Stewart once compared her to a china doll because Helen seemed so small and fragile. Helen thoroughly enjoyed being a wife and a mother, the traditional roles of women in the nineteenth century. Her husband was a successful businessman, and she was very happy to let him run their affairs. But a scorching day in July changed how Helen viewed her life forever.

Making a living in the dry Las Vegas Valley in 1884, with desert stretching in all directions, was difficult. But the Stewarts (husband Archibald, Helen, and four children) had acquired a home, Los Vegas Rancho, on a spring-fed creek, the only free-flowing water for miles. Cattle could be watered and crops grown, so the family prospered and the future looked bright, with Helen expecting a fifth child.

Helen often felt uneasy, however, about being left alone with four children while her husband traveled to sell beef and produce. With no banks nearby, their money was kept in an opening under a loose board above a window in the house. On July 13, 1884, a hired hand named Schyler Henry stormed in while Archibald was away on a trip, selling to the hungry miners in Eldorado Canyon southeast of the ranch. Henry told Helen he was quitting and demanded his wages. Helen was not going to reveal where their money was hidden, so she informed him he would have to wait for her husband's return in order to receive his pay. Henry grew menacing and bullied her to pay him. Although Helen felt intimidated, she did not back down, and he finally left to wait at a nearby ranch. Archibald returned a few days later. Although he was hot, dust-covered, and tired from his long ride in a freight wagon, Helen's story about how she had felt threatened—by what she later labeled a "black-hearted slanderer's tongue"—angered him. After a quick meal and rest, he left the house with his rifle and headed to the Kiel Ranch located a little over a mile away.

Exactly what happened that day is still a mystery, but Archibald was fatally shot in the head and chest. Helen learned of her husband's death when the ranch owner, Conrad Kiel, sent a note telling her to "send a team and take Mr. Sturd away—he is dead." In a letter to her attorney, Helen later described what she did:

> I left my little children with Mr. Frazier and went as fast as a horse could carry me. The man that killed my husband ran as I approached. As I got to the corner of the house I said oh where is he, oh where is he, and the Old Man Kiel and Hank Parrish said here he is and lifting a blanket showed me the lifeless form of my husband. I knelt beside him took his hand placed my hand upon his heart and looked upon his face and saw a bullet hole about two inches above the temple . . . . (Letter to George Sawyer, July 16, 1884).

No lumber could be found to make a coffin, so Helen resorted to using the doors from the ranch house. Archibald was buried the next day in an area that became the family cemetery and was called Four Acres.

Conrad Kiel and Schyler Henry were charged with the murder of Archibald Stewart. A trial was held about 108 miles away in Pioche, the location of the nearest courthouse in Lincoln County. A third man, Hank Parrish, disappeared the day of the murder and escaped prosecution. The all-male jury listened to the testimony of Helen, Kiel, and Henry, the only witnesses called. With no impartial witness, no decision could be reached; it was Helen's word against the statements of the men. The verdict brought no comfort to Helen or her children.

Because Archibald had left no will, Helen had to go to court to get ownership of the 960-acre ranch. The property was divided, with half given to her and the other half shared by the children. Usually, a widow received a $1,000 tax exemption from the Lincoln County Board of Equalization. Helen was granted this, but in effect gained nothing because the county commissioners raised the taxes on the Stewart ranch by $1,000 at the same meeting. Helen would either have to familiarize herself with the day-to-day operations of the ranch or sell it. She remembered what her husband had told her— Los Vegas Rancho was only supposed to be a temporary stop in their lives because she preferred living close to people. Helen agonized over the decision.

———•••———

Born in Springfield, Illinois, on April 16, 1854, to Hiram and Delia Gray Wiser, Helen had watched her mother care for the children while Helen's father worked. The family moved to Iowa, where they lived for two years while Hiram prospected in the Rocky Mountains. Helen and her sisters, Rachel (1855) and Aseneth (1857), were joined by twins, Henry and Flora, in 1863. When she was nine, Helen headed west with her family in a wagon train traveling through Carson Valley, Nevada, and then on to Galt, California, located south of Sacramento. She lived in a large two-story house that her father had purchased in Maine, dismantled, shipped around Cape Horn, and reconstructed in Galt. Helen attended school in Sacramento County and was a student at Hesperian College in Yolo County from 1867 to 1868. She earned a college degree, which was an unusual accomplishment for a woman at that time.

When she was eighteen, Helen married thirty-eight-year-old Archibald Richard Stewart, a naturalized citizen from Ireland who owned a flourishing freight business in Nevada. The wedding, which took place on April 6, 1873, in Stockton, California, fulfilled her parents' dream that she marry a successful older man. Helen, on the other hand, just liked that Archibald was tall and handsome. They moved to a remote cattle ranch at Pony Springs in Lincoln County, Nevada, about thirty miles north of Pioche, a bustling mining town founded in 1868 that became the county seat in 1871. Their first child, William James, was born there on March 9, 1874. Missing female companionship, especially during childbirth, Helen pleaded with Archibald to move them into Pioche, where over seven thousand people resided in an 1872 tally. Archibald continued to deal in cattle, opening a butcher shop in the town to sell his meat.

Now comfortably settled among many neighbors and informed of their activities by the *Pioche Daily News*, Helen gave birth to Hiram Richard on November 28, 1875. A third child, Flora Eliza Jane (known as "Tiza") followed on January 18, 1879. A close friend of Helen's later noted that Helen "loved being with people. She enjoyed hearing their footsteps, their voices and their laughter as they passed by her home—things she had missed in those lonely dreary years at Pony Springs. That was an experience she did not care to live over again."

When a business acquaintance, Octavius Decatur Gass, could not pay the taxes on his ranch in 1879, Archibald loaned him $5,000 in gold and took as collateral the isolated 640-acre Los Vegas Rancho. Gass used this spelling so it wouldn't be confused with Las Vegas, New Mexico, another settlement about five hundred miles east. Gass planned to use money from his next year's crops to pay off the loan, but bad weather wiped them out. Gass could not repay the loan, and Archibald foreclosed. Gass signed over his ranch plus an additional 320 acres and 1,500 cows, horses, mules, and sheep. Seeing potential in the new place, Archibald moved his family to the Las Vegas Valley in 1882. Helen, pregnant once more, did not want to leave her community of friends, but her husband promised the move was temporary—it would only be until they found another buyer for the land. To Helen's dismay, the Stewart family would once again be living on a ranch in a desolate area.

Los Vegas Rancho was on the site of an old adobe fort built in 1855. Brigham Young, a Mormon leader, had wanted a mission established between Salt Lake City, Utah, and the Pacific Coast, but the mission only operated for two years. After purchasing the property in 1865, Gass had used part of the foundation, the walls of the southwest corner of the old fort, and some of the other adobe buildings to build the flat-roofed, single-story ranch house that contained a kitchen, bedroom, and living room. He completed the modest home in 1873 and lived there with his wife, Mary Virginia Simpson, a niece of Ulysses S. Grant, who was then President of the United States (1869–1877).

From the house to the distant surrounding mountains, all one could see were sand and desert plants, but cool water bubbled from a natural underground well. After the Stewarts moved in, the ranch house was expanded with a new wing of two bedrooms and a porch was added to both the east and west sides of the house. Although the alkaline soil made growing crops a challenge, fruit (peaches, pears, apples, and figs) and vegetables (corn, beans, beets, and cabbage) matured and were sold to the miners in the camps in southern Nevada. Helen developed several new kinds of fruit trees suited to the desert environment and is said to have used the fruit to make holiday jam. Grapes were plentiful, and a good harvest could yield six hundred gallons of wine. Horses, cattle, and other livestock were also raised. Buyers from as far away as Wyoming made the ten-day ride to purchase their cattle.

The ranch became a way station for folks traveling between southern California and Salt Lake City. Meadows shaded by huge cottonwood trees provided spots where travelers could find relief from the sizzling Mojave Desert sun and temperatures as hot as 117 degrees. Clouds of dust in the distance would announce the impending arrival of weary visitors, giving Helen time to prepare fresh coffee and biscuits to share. She looked forward to the company and urged them to stay as long as they wanted. Another daughter, Evaline "Eva" La Vega, was born on September 22, 1882. Her middle name reflects her birth on the ranch.

After Archibald's death on July 13, 1884, Helen made up her mind and boldly took charge. With the help of her father, children, local Paiutes, and hired workers, she managed the day-by-day operations of the ranch. She also gave birth to her fifth child, Archibald Stewart, on January 25, 1885. He was named for his father and people called him "Archie." After his birth, people might have encountered Helen outside, in a beautifully fitted dress and heavy work boots, ready to tackle a needed task.

When rumors began to spread about a railroad coming through the area, Helen purchased more land, expanding her holdings to include more than eighteen hundred acres with water rights. Being the largest landowner in Lincoln County, her ranch became a center of activity in the region. A polling precinct was established there in 1890, and the ranch became the voting site. People traveled there to pick up their mail because the ranch housed the first official Las Vegas post office in 1893, with Helen serving as the postmistress until 1903. The Postal Service continued the "Los Vegas" spelling until 1903, when it was changed to its current spelling of Las Vegas, which is Spanish for "the meadows."

Although Helen kept Four Acres—where her husband as well as her son Archie (who was killed in a riding accident in July 1899) were buried—in 1902, she sold the rest of the ranch and some water rights for $55,000 to Senator William Andrews Clark of the San Pedro, Los Angeles & Salt Lake Railroad, later known as the Union Pacific. The value of that income today would equal over $3 million. The company built a railroad linking Salt Lake City and southern California. The first day of operation on the Salt Lake-to-Los Angeles route was May 1, 1905. Helen was given a complimentary rail pass for use in 1906.

The railroad then sold the remaining 110 acres of vacant land that it owned. This land sale, in what is today known as downtown Las Vegas, is credited as the beginning of the city. On May 15, 1905, half of the twelve hundred plots of land were auctioned by the railroad company to about two thousand eager but sweltering buyers. The temperature soared to over one hundred degrees that day. About the same number of lots were put up for auction the next day. Some lots sold for $100, while corner commercial lots garnered $1,750.

With the arrival of the railroad in the area and people now owning property, it was inevitable that the population would increase as jobs were created and houses built. The town installed electricity and local phone service in 1906. Today, Las Vegas is part of Clark County, which was created in 1909 and named for the wealthy businessman and Montana senator who brought the railroad to the area. As Helen described the change: "Following the trail of the trapper and of the trail blazer, and the pioneer, came the iron horse, that great annihilator of time and distance, bringing all the modern ideas of advanced civilization in our midst and we awoke as if in a dream and found all the comforts of an advanced civilization with us. The hardships were no more."

The sale of the ranch did not put an end to Helen's desire to own land and watch Las Vegas grow. She bought 280 acres near Four Acres and decided to build a new house. She and her family stayed in Los Angeles, California, during its construction. In 1903, while living there, Helen's son Hiram caught a cold after swimming and died when it turned into pneumonia. His body was returned and buried at Four Acres.

On July 23, 1903, while still in the Los Angeles area, Helen remarried, this time to another Stewart but with no relation to Archibald. Frank Royer Stewart had worked on her ranch since 1886. Helen insisted on a prenuptial agreement that stipulated her children would inherit her money and land. In 1903, men still usually held control of family resources, so Helen again broke society's norms with this decision. She had learned a lot about property rights from having to fight to keep her property when Archibald died. Although Helen had used the name Mrs. Archie Stewart, she never became Mrs. Frank Stewart, instead choosing to be called Mrs. Helen J. Stewart.

Helen enjoyed watching the daily interactions of the people in Las Vegas. It was quickly becoming the social and business center of the area and she had greatly missed such urban experiences during her years of living in isolated places. On March 17, 1911, Governor Tasker Oddie signed the city charter for Las Vegas, and Helen was given the pen he used for this purpose. One of the first streets in Las Vegas was also named for the Stewart family and it remains a major thoroughfare in the city.

In 1916, Governor Emmet D. Boyle appointed Helen as a delegate to the annual Convention of the American Civic Association, to be held at the New Willard Hotel from December 13 to 15, 1916, in Washington DC. This organization's purpose was to improve living conditions in the United States. Helen valued education and wanted local children who couldn't afford a tutor or who went to southern California for schooling, like Tiza, Eva, and Archie had done, to have educational opportunities in Nevada. Helen was already of member of the Clark County School Board and in 1916 was elected to the state board of education.

Helen donated the land for the first school building in the city in 1922, and Las Vegas Grammar School Branch No. 1 opened on that land the following year. It was the first public school attended by students from the local Paiute tribe, and it operated until 1967. Helen would sometimes visit the school on picture day and be included in class photos. Known as the Historic Westside School, the building was placed on the National Register of Historic Places on April 2, 1979. An alternative public school that served elementary and high school special education students was named the Helen J. Stewart School for Helen's namesake granddaughter.

Helen worked with the Nevada Federation of Women's Clubs and helped found the Mesquite Club in 1911. Her many interactions with the local Paiute people had taught her much about their culture and she knew that they prized the mesquite tree for its many uses. Growing along rivers in the Southwest, the mesquite produces large edible bean pods. Its sap can be used as an antiseptic and a tea made from its leaves helps relieve headaches. Helen thought it would be a fitting name for a service organization and had the organizational gavel made from mesquite wood. One of the club's early achievements was providing the city with a library. Using the slogan "To plant a tree is to bless the earth," they also raised enough money to purchase two thousand cottonwood trees, which were planted throughout the town. Helen was elected club president in 1916. She also helped found the U-Wah-Un Study Club in 1919. The club's name means "circle of friends" in Paiute, and in addition to studying music and literature, this group gave nature books to local libraries.

Helen supported equal rights for women in various ways, including in 1922, when she served on the first jury in Clark County to include women. It was a murder trial, so Helen became one of the first women in Nevada to decide a murder case. This may have brought her a sense of solace concerning her husband's murder—now women would play an integral role in deciding such events. In 1908, when the southern division of the Nevada Historical Society was created, she served as its first president. Helen often shared her personal pioneer experiences and recollections about southern Nevada history with various civic groups. She was also a founding member of the Society of Nevada Pioneers, established on October 30, 1914.

Helen's great respect for the Paiute Indians motivated her to lobby federal agencies as early as 1895 for funds to educate the local indigenous people. In January 1912, the *Las Vegas Age* reported that Helen had sold ten acres of land to the federal government to be used as "an Indian school and semi-reservation." It was to be known as the Las Vegas Paiute Colony, and the property remains in tribal control today. Helen also acquired a large quantity of Indian baskets, jewelry, and other artifacts. The 550 baskets in her collection were considered to be the finest in Nevada, and Governor James G. Scrugham wanted to display them at the 1926 state exposition to be held in Reno. He suggested that the state buy them from her. Helen wanted the State of Nevada to have these items, as she had written in a 1919 note: "I have many things I would like to have preserved for future benefit to my Home and State. . . . I have spent much time and money in getting my collection as near perfect as I could. . . . I wish to place in book form that they may be together a History of a people that has lived nearer to God and Nature than any race of people on the face of the earth."

Although Helen did start writing about her artifacts, her project was never finished and the state never acquired her baskets. She was diagnosed with cancer in 1924 and had to take many trips to Los Angeles, California, for treatment. But as she wrote to her daughter Tiza: "Going to a Hospital makes quite a hole in ones Pocket Book but that is better than being Dead for when you are Dead you are Dead a long time."

Helen died in Las Vegas on March 6, 1926, almost eight years after Frank, who had died on September 1, 1918, at age sixty-seven. She was buried in the family burial plot. Her heirs decided to sell the basket collection to the Fred Harvey Company, which ran hotels along the Atchison, Topeka & Santa Fe Railroad, and whose tracks did not cross Nevada.

Las Vegas was devastated by Helen's passing. Businesses, schools, and even the Federal Post Office closed out of respect on the day of Helen's funeral. The streets were filled with people from all over the state and beyond who mourned the loss of this pioneer spirit. According to her obituary, published on March 12, 1926, in the *Las Vegas Review-Journal*: "The largest funeral procession ever witnessed in Las Vegas wended its way from the house on the Stewart Ranch to the Church where the services were held."

In her seventy-two years, Helen proved that she was tough and could not be broken by physical isolation, death of loved ones, or

Helen J. Stewart with some of her baskets around 1910. —Helen J. Stewart Photo Collection [0104 007113]. UNLV Libraries Special Collections & Archives

41

unjust decisions by others. She dedicated herself to a place she originally believed she would only live in for a short while and that she thought she wouldn't like. But the desert caught her heart, as she noted in a letter to her daughter Tiza in October 1924: "I would like to be in an Auto with a good driver and away out over the Desert. Just to ride and Ride away the hours til the night then home again."

To celebrate her accomplishments, a life-size bronze statue of Helen was erected in 2011 at the Old Las Vegas Mormon Fort State Historic Park, which preserves the site of Helen's original home. Created by Benjamin Victor, the statue was unveiled on December 3, 2011, and portrays her in a fancy dress and work boots. Around her feet are objects that were important in her lifetime: mesquite bush, Paiute baskets, letters from her time as postmaster, and the Episcopal Common Prayer book for her efforts in founding Christ Episcopal Church, which still exists. Helen is often the subject of park ranger presentations for visitors to the fort.

Today, the members of the Stewart family still rest together, but they are no longer buried at Four Acres. In the 1970s, that land was purchased by Bunker Brothers Mortuary, and all of the remains were relocated to Bunkers Eden Vale Memorial Park, which is located on North Las Vegas Boulevard, very close to the site of the original Stewart family home.

In 1938 while staying at the Sal Sagev (Las Vegas spelled backwards) Hotel, Helen's daughter Tiza wrote a brief memoir about her mother. In it, she noted that, for many years, Helen Jane Wiser Stewart literally "lived by the side of the road and was a friend to man." Known as the "First Lady of Las Vegas," she laid the groundwork for the city in many ways. Although Helen thought of herself as a historian, and this was the occupation listed on her death certificate, she was a history maker as well.

4

FELICE COHN
(about 1878–1961)

US Supreme Court
Welcomes Woman No. 4

In many types of competitive events, people often strive to earn first, second, or third place and may be disgruntled if they don't achieve one of these recognitions. However, Felice Cohn was elated to be number four. On February 15, 1879, the US Congress approved the following language, which President Rutherford B. Hayes signed into law:

> That any woman who shall have been a member of the bar of the highest court of any State or Territory or of the Supreme Court of the District of Columbia for the space of three years, and shall have maintained a good standing before such court, and who shall be a person of good moral character, shall, on motion, and the production of such record, be admitted to practice before the Supreme Court of the United States.

The first woman to be admitted to practice law before the US Supreme Court was Belva Ann Lockwood, who obtained a law degree from National University Law School (now the George Washington University Law School) in Washington DC on March 3, 1879. She became the first woman to argue a case (*Kaiser v. Stickney*) in front of the justices late in 1880. Her most famous case before the Supreme Court was *United States v. Cherokee Nation*. She argued on

Felice Cohn, circa 1932. —Press photo

behalf of the Eastern Cherokee in a case centering on a debt owed to the tribe by the US government. In 1906, Belva won a $5 million settlement for the Cherokee.

Ada Bittenbender, from Nebraska, followed in October 1888. Vermont's Myra Colby Bradwell received her license to practice before the Supreme Court on March 28, 1892. At a Washington DC ceremony in March 1916, Felice Cohn became the fourth woman allowed to practice law before the US Supreme Court. She met President Woodrow Wilson at a White House reception when, keeping the elite of Washington society waiting, he stopped to commend Felice for achieving what few women had in that era: appointment as a Supreme Court attorney. When she was admitted to the Nevada bar in 1902, through the Ninth District of the US District Court in Carson City, it had only been nine years since Nevada allowed women to practice law. All of this occurred well before women were granted the right to vote in 1920 via the Nineteenth Amendment. Its passage heralded a societal change for American women, but change in the legal field occurred slowly.

In 1931, Felice was still the only practicing female attorney in Nevada. By 1947, 175 attorneys practiced law in Reno, but only three were women: Charlotte Hunter Arley, Margaret Bailey, and Felice. Why were women so hesitant to enter this male-dominated profession and what motivated Felice Cohn to stay?

———•••———

As is the case with many records in the nineteenth century, there seems to be confusion about when Felice Cohn was born. The 1880 US Census reported that she was born in 1878, as did the 1900 census. In 1910, however, her age was given as twenty-eight, which would make her birth year 1882. According to her Nevada death record, Felice was born on May 18, 1884. However, the 1878 date seems most likely given her presence in the 1880 census and her high school graduation date of 1894. The fact that the 1884 date has sometimes been used to calculate her age seems to have fostered the belief in some accounts of her life that she was a child prodigy.

All sources agree that she was born in Carson City—the daughter of Morris and Pauline Sheyer Cohn—both of whom had been born in Prussia, which was part of Germany, and immigrated to the United States. According to Felice's father's obituary, he came to the United States when he was fourteen years old and to Nevada in 1868. Her maternal grandfather was Jacob Sheyer, the Polish-born rabbi of the local synagogue. After living for a while in Marysville, California, he brought his family to Carson City in 1863. In 1872, the *Daily State Register* of that city called him the "Rabbi for the State of Nevada." Rabbi Sheyer died in April 1875, and that same year Pauline married Morris. In the 1880 US Census, Morris is listed as a merchant; his obituary, reprinted in the *Nevada Appeal* in 2005, defined his occupation as owner of a dry goods store in Carson City. The eligible voter records of 1870 for Hamilton in White Pine County show that Morris and his brother Alexander also ran a tobacco store; it sold Havana cigars and cutlery, but was lost in a fire in 1873. Morris's obituary also notes: "He engaged in mining ventures at times and once held extensive ranching interests in Carson Valley, where he established the first creamery and was also active getting alfalfa growing started in the valley."

Morris reportedly owned more than eight thousand acres in Carson Valley and the Lake Tahoe area. In 1897, Governor Reinhold Sadler picked him to be part of a plan to expand Nevada's population with East European Jewish colonists. The Hebrew Agricultural Society of the United States requested that Nevada help Polish, Russian, and Austrian Jews settle in the state. While that venture, which was known as the Occidental Colony Company, did not triple the number of residents in the state as hoped, it does demonstrate that Morris Cohn was viewed as a powerful man and his family enjoyed a somewhat lavish lifestyle. For example, Chinese cooks and servants were employed to help Pauline with household chores.

Felice, her brother Herbert (born 1885), and three sisters, Bertha (1876), Tichelle (1882), and Lillian (1888), all attended school in Carson City. Felice graduated from Carson High School in 1894. She may have considered entering the medical field because she reportedly had numerous great uncles who were doctors. However, Felice decided she "would rather argue than prescribe." She went on to Nevada Normal School (now University of Nevada, Reno) and Stanford University in Palo Alto, California. The Stanford University Alumni Directory confirms that Felice attended the university during the years 1895 to 1897. She is also listed in the 1898 *Quad* yearbook as a participant in the Roble Mandolin Club, where she is identified as a second mandolin player scheduled to graduate in the spring of 1900. However, there is no evidence that she actually graduated from Stanford. It is documented that between 1894 and 1903 she earned three teaching credentials from her work at these institutions, and it is reported that she worked as a teacher for a short while.

As far as we know, Felice's first foray into law was when she took some classes at Washington Law School (now Washington University School of Law) in St. Louis, Missouri. The *Virginia City Evening Chronicle* reported on July 24, 1893, that the Nevada Legislature passed a law that year that gave women the same rights and privileges as men "so far as becoming attorneys is concerned." Twenty-two-year-old Laura May Tilden, who studied law with her father, became Nevada's first female attorney when she passed the bar on July 23, 1893. Felice was admitted to practice law in Nevada on June 17, 1902. She is recognized as the first woman born in Nevada to practice law in the state, the fifth woman admitted to the Nevada bar, the first female Jewish attorney, and the first woman to actually have formal legal training in law in order to practice. Felice must also have been licensed in California, because her name appears on the official state record, *California, Occupational Licenses, Registers, and Directories, 1876–1969* as follows: "12 May 1908, Attorney, Roll of Attorneys/District Court of Appeal, First District, Volume 1, admitted by motion." Felice also later received a legal license in Colorado.

While Felice lived at 104 Henry Street in Carson City, she shared a law office in the State Bank Building with Samuel Platt, also from a prosperous Jewish family with a German heritage. He became her mentor and served in that role until the two later clashed over the issue of women's suffrage. He was appointed by President Theodore Roosevelt as US District Attorney for Nevada in 1906, and it is believed that Felice may have assisted him with some of his cases between 1906 and 1914.

In 1905, Felice headed to Goldfield in Esmeralda County to establish another office. Her father's interest in property acquisition probably led her to focus her practice on land disputes, acquiring patents on mining claims, and other issues related to mining. She arrived just as Goldfield boomed due to the local gold strikes at the foot of Columbia Mountain, becoming the largest city in Nevada. At an altitude of almost six thousand feet, life in Goldfield during her six-month stay probably tested her mettle as she joined the eighteen thousand to twenty thousand people who crowded the streets and stores.

Newspaper accounts record that there were sixty saloons in the town. When a fire broke out on July 8, 1905, the beer found a different purpose. The *Tonopah Daily Sun* reported the next day: "The buildings of the Enterprise Mercantile Company were saved by the free and unlimited use of beer. Barrel after barrel was used and had a most desirous effect. Had it not been for the liquid the entire stock of goods of the company would have been ruined."

Felice was somewhat of an oddity in this freewheeling mining town because she was neither looking for a husband nor speculating in stocks, and she practiced law alongside many male lawyers. Even they found the conditions in Goldfield challenging that year: "A fellow who takes one of the boom camps . . . must . . . carry his library and possessions in a suit case and trunk. . . . He may be called

Goldfield, sometime between 1905 and 1908. —Library of Congress, photograph by Per Edward Larss

on to draft an important conveyance on a poker table without blank forms, typewriter or scarcely legal-cap paper, but if he picks the right place . . . he ought to succeed if he sticks to it."

Felice might have met the Earps, who participated in the 1881 gunfight at the OK Corral in Tombstone, Arizona. Virgil Earp was a county deputy sheriff that year in Goldfield. His brother Wyatt was a pit boss at the Northern Saloon, whose lengthy bar took eighty bartenders to keep up with the thirsty and often rowdy patrons. In 1907, a curious reporter for the *Goldfield Daily Tribune* asked Felice why a woman would choose to become an attorney. She responded, "I have a great liking for the law and I find it entirely within a woman's powers." The reporter noted in the August 15 article:

"There is nothing about her appearance or manner to suggest that she is at all masculine nor . . . that would suggest that she was other than a well reared woman of refined taste." It described her as a "slender woman of average height, with dark hair and liquid black eyes, which flash with interest as she talks." Because of her work in Goldfield, Felice became known as an expert in mining and corporate law in the western states. She traveled all over that region, and for several years she maintained an office in Denver, Colorado. Felice was not intimidated by arguing a case before an all-male jury. Ironically, Felice could not have served on a jury herself; Nevada prohibited women from serving in that role until 1918.

In 1907, Felice agreed to serve as the court reporter for Ormsby County in the State Bank & Trust Company case. The bank loaned funds to a land speculating company in Tonopah, and when that company failed, so did the bank, which was then sued. One wonders why Felice opted to accept this position, because her law practice was successful, but she must have known that her talents would prove useful in sorting through the mass of evidence presented in the four-year trial—one of the longest in state history. Testimony from one witness lasted 147 days. Felice liked the work and did that as well as practice law for eight years.

On May 12, 1908, Felice was admitted to the District Court of Appeals in San Francisco. During World War I (1914–1918), she left her law practice in Nevada and worked for the federal government as Assistant Superintendent of Public Land Sales. In her later campaigning for public office, as she stated in the *Nevada State Journal* on May 1, 1927, she took on this responsibility so that the four men who were working the job could join the military. The knowledge she had acquired about mining in Goldfield helped her as she supervised land sales and mineral claims between the government and the Southern Pacific and Union Pacific Railroads. During the war, Felice was also admitted to practice law before the US Supreme Court. From March to May of 1916, she was feted with invitations to events in Washington DC as well as New York. Hometown newspapers in Reno touted that Felice was becoming "the center of attention" in Washington.

In 1918, as the first woman to be a special hearings attorney for the US Land Office, she handled land fraud cases in Nevada, Colorado, Oklahoma, and Kansas. She left this position in 1922, happy that she had restored over eighty thousand acres of land to the public domain.

As a professional woman, Felice was an early participant in the Nevada suffrage movement. Her legal knowledge helped her draft the women's suffrage resolution that was introduced to the state legislature by Assemblymen Emory J. Arnold and J. F. Byrne on January 31, 1911. She addressed the Nevada legislature about voting rights for women, and the bill passed the assembly in March of that year. It stated: "There shall be no denial of the elective franchise at any election on account of sex." She served as President of the Non-Militant Equal Suffrage Association from 1912 to 1914, after pulling away from the Nevada Equal Franchise Society, which she felt was too aggressive. An article in the July 31, 1913, edition of the national magazine *Leslie's Weekly* stated: "and like the great majority of woman suffragists in this country, [Felice Cohn] does not believe in militant methods."

Drawing upon her earlier effort, Felice wrote the 1914 resolution—which the legislature took under consideration—to amend the Nevada Constitution to allow women the right to vote. This time, it passed both houses. In 1916, one hundred people joined her in Washington DC to lobby for the suffrage amendment at the national level. She chided the nation in an essay entitled, "Women of Nevada Interested In Politics," in which she wrote that Nevada women enjoyed more freedom than those who lived elsewhere and "appear much like the lives of our sisters in other states—broadened and sweetened, mayhap, by the splendid liberty that is ours." Nevada women were able to vote well before August 18, 1920, when the

Nineteenth Amendment to the US Constitution granted all American women that right.

Felice entered private practice in Reno in 1921 with an office in the Mapes Building. For years, her ad in the *Reno Gazette-Journal* listed her as:

MISS FELICE COHN—ATTORNEY AT LAW
14-15 Chas. W. Mapes Building, formerly Gray-Reid Building, Phone 8441
(As found in September 13, 1934 issue).

She soon assumed another job as US Referee in Bankruptcy for Nevada, a position she held from 1926 to 1934. She was one of the first women given such an appointment. Only two of her rulings were overturned—an exceedingly strong record. Her refusal to be a witness in the bankruptcy case against the Owl Drug Store Company, which some politicians considered a ploy to defraud stockholders, may have led to her not being reappointed to the role in 1934. However, Felice rebounded when she was appointed as the national chair for the Committee on Ethics, a working group of the National Association of Referees in Bankruptcy.

Felice opened her law practice in Reno just in time to participate in Nevada's divorce industry. In 1927, Nevada changed its residency requirements for a divorce from six months to three months. In 1931, the requirements were again reduced, this time to six weeks. During a speech in New York, Felice noted, "Nevada has been criticized for her divorce laws, but it is due almost entirely to the need of relief by the citizens of other states that we find ourselves the 'cure' center of the world. . . . They came to Nevada because the laws of their own states afforded no avenue of escape from an intolerable condition, brought about most often by incompatibility and nothing more."

Felice criticized the last decrease in residency change because having divorce seekers stay for three months benefited the local economy. She also felt that a longer waiting period might allow more reconciliation time for the couple. In addition, Felice supported a uniform divorce law for all states and advocated for that with her colleagues. She believed that the system that existed at the time led to the "absurdity of a person being single in one state, married in another, and a bigamist in still another, all at one and the same time." By 1933, however, she had handled over fifteen hundred divorce cases in five states (Nevada, California, Utah, Wyoming, and Colorado). Felice also pushed Nevada legislators to reform laws concerning child labor, adoption, and the regulations for foster homes. She vehemently opposed any legislation where women and children were negatively affected.

Felice decided to try the political arena in 1924, running unsuccessfully for state assembly on the Democratic ticket. Undeterred by that defeat, she campaigned in 1927 to be city attorney for Reno. Her platform, advocating for the divorce rights of women, was probably too liberal for many voters. She also ran for Washoe County District Judge in 1942, 1950, and 1952, but again, did not win the position. Felice kept reminding the Nevada women voters of what she had stated earlier in her essay: "[N]o matter how varied our tastes may be; no matter whether we be homemakers or business women, or perhaps both (for we frequently combine these talents); no matter whether we be young or old, rich or poor, active or ailing, we have one great interest that appeals to us all . . . . And that is Politics! Yes, Politics—capital "P" at that!"

No matter how busy she was, Felice always found time to participate in organizations that supported her career and beliefs. She was a member of the International Association of Women Lawyers, acted as Nevada vice president of the American Bar Association from 1930 to 1931, and was vice president of the National Association of Women Lawyers. She was a member of the Nevada and California Bar Associations as well as a member of the National Association of Referees in Bankruptcy. Felice was also a trustee on the board and served as the lawyer for the Reno Young Women's Christian Association. She chaired the legislative committee of the American Federation of Women's Clubs. As a founding member of the Nevada Federation of Business and Professional Women's Clubs in 1936, she also served as the first president. On May 24, 1950, this organization named Felice as the state's most outstanding woman for her efforts as an attorney and suffragette. Felice was also a member of the Iota Tau Tau sorority, an international sorority for women in the legal profession.

Concern for others led Felice to participate in a number of service and charitable groups. As the *Nevada State Journal* observed in 1932, "She still finds time to assist those organizations which sponsor welfare work and interest among all people." Felice orchestrated the campaign to raise funds for a headquarters for the Nevada Historical Society. Her efforts helped acquire a state grant of $15,000 for that purpose. She served on the American Red Cross board beginning in 1925, and for the next fifteen years, chaired the Home Service Committee, which provided monetary and material assistance for veterans and their families. During World War II, she supported the United Service Organizations. Being a native Nevadan, she helped start Nevada Native Daughters, a social organization dedicated to remembering and honoring the pioneers of the state. Felice participated in the Reno branch of the United Nations Association and served as president from 1930 to 1931. Felice was also extremely active in the B'nai B'rith Nevada Auxiliary No. 9, a Jewish community service organization, and served as the group's president in 1941.

Although Felice worked hard, she also allotted time for recreation in her life. In August 1934, she traveled to Honolulu, Hawaii, on the ship *Lurline*. Although in her fifties, she thoroughly enjoyed the tropical beauty of the islands well before Hawaii became a state in 1959. In February 1955, she traveled again by ship from Galveston, Texas, to the French Antilles in the Caribbean Sea. Still maintaining her law practice into her seventies, in 1957 she opted to travel around Europe for a year, possibly taking the "grand tour" many upper-class women of this period experienced as young girls—an opportunity that Felice had been too busy for at that age because she was focused on her career.

Felice suffered from arteriosclerosis for many years, which contributed to her death from a heart attack on May 24, 1961. Her body was cremated and buried at Mountain View Cemetery in Reno. It took the *Reno Evening Gazette* almost half of a column on the obituary page in that day's edition to overview all of her many accomplishments. Today, residents of Felice Cohn Court in Las Vegas continue to honor her memory with their choice of housing.

Because of the confusion around her birth date, or perhaps because local newspapers wanted to bolster the accomplishments of a hometown celebrity, some published material incorrectly portrays Felice as one possessing talents and abilities way beyond her years. However, these errors should not tarnish Felice's extraordinary record of distinguished public service and her lasting achievements on behalf of women's suffrage. Because she never married, Felice's life focused on her professional work. She opened many doors for Nevada women and was a national advocate for multiple social causes. As the *Nevada State Journal* commented in 1932, "With women taking their place in world affairs . . . and with Felice Cohn's background we dare not venture an opinion as to how far this outstanding daughter of Nevada may go." It turned out to be an apt prediction of what she would accomplish.

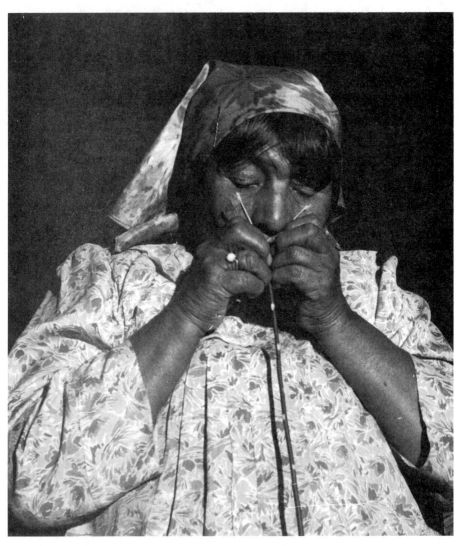

Wuzzie George splitting willows for baskets in Fallon. —Margaret M. Wheat Collection [UNRS-P1989-32-0179], University Libraries, Special Collections Department, University of Nevada, Reno

WUZZIE DICK GEORGE

(circa 1880–1984)

Guardian of the Old Ways

Although we usually only think of living things as becoming extinct, products, services, and traditions can also be lost over time. Gas stations used to hire people to put gasoline in cars for drivers, but now self-service gas is the norm. Pay phones used to be available in most public places, but they are few and far between now that the majority of people own personal cell phones. Taking photographs with a camera used to require buying rolls of film, but digital cameras no longer necessitate this purchase. Much writing used to be done on typewriters, but laptop computers now allow people to type long manuscripts at their convenience and emails have replaced handwritten letters.

Wuzzie Dick George was afraid that her people's native customs would be lost in a similar manner. As a child, she had learned tribal customs and traditions from her Northern Paiute grandmother. When she was gone, who would remember how her people lived and instruct others in the Paiutes' ways? The Northern Paiutes were divided into bands. Who would know the differences between the Jackrabbit-eaters and the Trout-eaters or any of the other twenty-three bands that comprised the Northern Paiute tribes of Nevada, California, Idaho, and Oregon? This bothered Wuzzie and she vowed to find a way to do something to preserve the heritage of her people.

———•••———

The actual date of Wuzzie Dick's birth is a big mystery. While it is often reported as occurring between 1880 and 1883, the US Indian Census for 1924 and other years records her year of birth as 1895. The US Social Security Death Index lists her date of birth as March 1, 1883, but because Wuzzie recounted that she was born during "pine nut time," it is doubtful that she was born in March, because pine nut season usually means September or October in northern Nevada. Records also suggest that her father had to break ice in order to take the traditional bath of a Paiute father when a child is born, so Wuzzie's birth had to have been during or close to late fall through early spring.

Her father's Paiute name was Tohakusa, but he had been given the name Sam Dick by a white employer. Her mother was Suzie Dick. Both were members of the Northern Paiute tribe. Suzie was Sam's second wife; he had previously married her older sister Mattie, who was named for their mother. Having multiple wives was allowed in Paiute culture. Sam and Suzie Dick gave their baby the Paiute name "WizPi," which means small animal, perhaps inspired by the woods where her parents were gathering pine nuts. "Wuzzie" is the most frequent spelling of her name, although the US Bureau of Indian Affairs census records list her as "Wassie" and "Woozie." Wuzzie had two half sisters, Mammie and Maggie, and a younger sister named Josephine.

As a child, Wuzzie lived near what was known as Indian Village, about sixty miles east of present-day Reno near the Carson Desert, named after frontiersman Kit Carson. Fallon, which is the current county seat of Churchill County, is located in the area where Wuzzie spent most of her life. Her father, Sam, was employed as a general ranch hand by Charles Kaiser. Sam tended flocks of sheep, built fences, and did whatever else was needed to keep the ranch functioning. Kaiser always paired him with a white work partner, which is how Sam learned to speak English. Wuzzie's mother washed dishes at a hotel run by John Sanford in Stillwater, today a ghost town in Churchill County. Consequently, Wuzzie was most often cared for by her grandparents, Pawigiadi (who was known as "Stovepipe") and Yabatoniga (Mattie). Her grandfather died when she was a small child, so Wuzzie learned the traditions and customs of her tribe mostly from Mattie. Wuzzie's most prominent memory of her grandfather was that he was a good hunter who made obsidian arrowheads, often eating the chips of the shiny black volcanic rock that broke off during the construction because he believed they made him strong and powerful.

Wuzzie and Mattie generally started each day by collecting greasewood, a plentiful thorny shrub that can grow up to eight feet tall. In order to avoid paying fifteen cents for breakfast at the hotel where Suzie worked, they bartered the greasewood for food. Greasewood burned cleanly, and for a long time, in the kitchen stove. If they had any greasewood left, they made digging sticks for harvesting roots. They also used the wood for its medicinal properties. If an insect bit Wuzzie, she would crush some of the leaves and place them on the itchy spot. Their breakfast was served outside the back door of the hotel. Although it was early, they ate quickly because they had a lot to do. As Wuzzie recalled, "We never stay home. Just eat in the morning, don't take any food, and eat at night when we get home."

Wherever they went, they walked, because Stovepipe and Mattie did not own a horse. If it was summer, Mattie might have collected grubs from the roots of the greasewood to take home and roast. Wuzzie thought they tasted greasy. Wuzzie caught fish in the rivers and lakes using handmade single-barbed harpoons. She and her grandmother would also gather berries. Her band of people was known as "Cattail-eaters" because they dug cattails out of the low-lying land along the Carson River. The white cores of the roots were baked in hot coals and eaten or dried and ground into flour. The young shoots at the base of the leaf clusters were either eaten boiled or consumed raw. Mattie taught her to leave an offering—such as a small piece of cloth or a stone—when gathering roots, so that the plants would come back again the following year.

In September and October, Wuzzie looked forward to gathering pinyon pine nuts with other Paiutes. Pine nuts, an important food source for her people during the "starving time" of the winter, are about the size of olive pits and can be roasted and ground into flour. Their fall harvest was a social event looked forward to by all. Wuzzie explained the tradition of the harvest in her later recollections of her childhood: "When we come to a pinenut place we talk to the ground and the mountain and everything. We ask to feel good and strong . . . . The pinenuts belong to the mountain so we ask the mountain for some of its pinenuts to take home and eat."

Ducks were plentiful along the Carson River, especially in the spring, so Mattie showed Wuzzie how to gather duck eggs, which she placed in a special "egg bag" made of tule (reeds). While boiled eggs were often eaten at night, her grandmother buried extra ones in cool, moist sand to preserve them. Wuzzie's father, Sam, learned how to make a small wattle dugout, used for preservation, from his coworkers on the ranch. Thin branches were woven between upright stakes to form a lattice. This frame was then covered with daub, a primitive plaster probably made from sand, clay, and dried grass. The finished structure was placed over a hole in the ground to help keep food from spoiling. Being a good hunter, Sam sometimes added variety to their diet by bringing duck, geese, mudhens (today known as American coots), and wild pigs to be preserved or eaten immediately.

Other types of useful containers were made from reeds, cattails, and willow. In order to carry water, Mattie showed Wuzzie how to make finely woven willow jugs. When coated with red clay and hot pitch made from the sap of pine trees, they hardly leaked and the water stayed cooler. Cold water was a welcome treat on a sizzling summer day in the desert. Some jugs were big enough to hold five gallons of water. Baskets of all shapes and sizes were necessary for carrying and cooking food. Wuzzie watched Mattie make cooking baskets and helped her tie green willow twigs into stirring sticks. Cooking baskets would burn if placed directly on the fire, so Mattie cooked by dropping hot rocks into liquid to get it to boil in the cooking basket. Tightly woven baskets were needed for gathering seeds, especially the small, black seeds from Indian rice-grass, a food staple of Wuzzie's people. More loosely woven winnowing baskets helped separate unwanted items, such as dirt and insects, from the collected edibles.

Wuzzie also learned how to make mats and bags from tule and sagebrush bark, blankets from rabbit skins, and clothing and shoes from plant fibers. However, much of her daily clothing was made from store-bought fabric. By this time, Paiute women did not often wear the traditional buckskin, reed, and bark clothing, opting instead for loose-fitting calico dresses that they usually wore with a shawl and headscarf.

It was while they worked that Mattie taught Wuzzie about her heritage. Wuzzie remembered being told this story: "Before the [1860] war at Pyramid Lake, the Indians lived in tule houses for miles along the Carson Slough. Indians lived everyplace. Smoke all over when Indians built their fires in morning. When the soldiers threw poison in river lots of them died. My people stay in the mountains that time. That's what my grandma and grandpa always say."

Sometime between 1891 and 1893, Wuzzie's parents decided to separate. Her mother went to work on the Ernst Ranch, located on the Old River north of Fallon, and took ten-year-old Wuzzie with her. George Ernst was a state senator from 1896 to 1900 who owned considerable real estate and mining interests in the area. Ernst Drive still exists in Fallon. Wuzzie had to work for her keep at the ranch, so she ironed towels and other wrinkled cloth items. Because she was so small, Wuzzie needed to stand on a box in order to reach the ironing board. Tending a flock of sheep got her back outside. She received ten cents per day for her efforts, which mostly went toward purchases of sweet treats at Jim Richard's store, which was located in "Jim's Town." The store was close to Mike and Eliza Fallon's ranch house, built in 1896, which also became the first post office. The Paiute people bought clothes and flour at the store. This locale would become the town of Fallon and, in 1903, the county seat of Churchill County.

Although George Ernst and his wife, Ellen Mary, had seven children, all were teenagers or older by the time Wuzzie came to live with them. Ellen, who was probably glad to have a child in the house again, would talk to Wuzzie while she worked. As a result, Wuzzie learned to speak some English words.

While there are documents that state her mother's death led her father to remove Wuzzie from the Ernst Ranch when she was "a big girl," as she recalled, other records seem to contradict this belief. According to the US Indian Census (1933–1934) for the Walker River Agency, Suzie Dick lived until May 24, 1933, when she died of an inflammation in her digestive tract. Wuzzie's father supposedly took Wuzzie to stay with his mother in Virginia City, but she wasn't there for long. Calvin H. Ashbury, superintendent of the Stewart Indian School in Carson City from 1903 to 1912, escorted her to that boarding school, making Wuzzie one of the over thirty thousand Indian children who attended the school before it closed in 1980. The state government established the school and then sold it to the US Bureau of Indian Affairs for the purpose of educating children from many tribes and assimilating them into the mainstream culture. While the children were taught the three Rs (reading, writing, and arithmetic) at this off-reservation school, vocational training was emphasized.

During the six months Wuzzie was there (probably between 1903 and 1904), Wuzzie attended classes geared specifically for girls—baking, cooking, sewing and washing clothes, and the basics of nursing. When the school experienced a measles epidemic, her father removed her for fear she would contract the disease. Wuzzie was just starting to adjust to the rigid school schedule and expand her English language skills. Later she stated that she was sorry to have "lost my schooling." Sam took her back to Fallon and she lived with her half-sister, Mammie, and Mattie, her grandmother. Wuzzie completed the five-day traditional girl's rite of passage to womanhood at this time, which meant that she was of a marriageable age.

The name "Woozie" Springer appears in the 1909 US Bureau of Indian Affairs census records. It seems that Wuzzie married Joe Springer and that they had two children, Johnny and Julia. However, the couple divorced at some point between 1909 and 1912, and the children stayed with their father. In late 1909 or early 1910, Wuzzie took a job washing dishes at a restaurant in Fallon. A Chinese man named Goee owned this establishment, which was popular with the Paiute men working in the area. Here, Wuzzie met Jimmie (also spelled Jimmy) George, who was working in John Oats' hay fields. Unfortunately, Wuzzie lost her job when, along with many of the other wooden buildings in the downtown area of Fallon, the restaurant burned on May 19, 1910. Luckily, Marge Harmon's house in Fallon was spared and she hired Wuzzie for household chores. Wuzzie and Jimmie got married.

Jimmie was born sometime between 1875 and 1879. He was probably Western Shoshone through his father's line and Northern Paiute by his mother. She died when he was a baby, and he was raised by her mother. Like Wuzzie, he learned a lot about the ways of his ancestors from a grandparent.

Wuzzie and Jimmie had eight children: Naomi (1914); Freddy (1915); Winona (c. 1916); Leonard (c. 1921); Gladys (1924); Walter (1926); Ivan (1929); and Ashley (1933). Naomi and Freddy died very young, and Gladys died at age sixteen from complications with pneumonia. Wuzzie continued working for Mrs. Harmon off and on until about 1928, when they moved to the local reservation so that Winona and Leonard could go to school.

Sometime between 1915 and 1920, Jimmie killed a deer. That night, he dreamed about the deer and believed he was being given its power. He consulted Calico George, a native doctor who validated him as a medicine man. Jimmie began treating breathing problems and the painful swelling of sprains and stiff joints. Other dreams of eagles, hummingbirds, and mountain rattlesnakes expanded his medical powers. Reportedly, hummingbirds would land on him as a sign of his abilities. In his medicine bag, he kept items that represented these powers, such as the skin of a hummingbird and a rattle made from a deer's dewclaws.

People would send for Jimmie, and he and Wuzzie would sometimes travel up to four days, initially by wagon and later by automobile, to reach the patient. Jimmie would go into a trance to determine the cause of the person's illness, and Wuzzie acted as his interpreter. It is estimated that he treated about a thousand people before he stopped practicing in the 1950s, when he lost the hummingbird skin in his doctoring kit. Being a medicine man had never been a profitable occupation for Jimmie, but both he and Wuzzie were sad when he lost his powers.

In the 1950s, Jimmie and Wuzzie met Margaret Marean Wheat, a self-taught anthropologist interested in documenting the lifestyle of the Paiute tribes of northern Nevada. Peg, as she was known, interviewed many tribal elders and recorded their conversations, as well as old songs and prayers, with a wire recorder. She also took still photos with a box camera. After receiving a grant from the Fleischmann Foundation of Nevada, she was able to purchase the supplies she needed, including more sophisticated equipment. She hired Jimmie and Wuzzie as consultants, and they received a small stipend. In 1964, Peg acquired the help of Dave Nichols, who worked at the University of Nevada, Reno in audio-visual services. He filmed Jimmie and Wuzzie as they demonstrated Paiute activities such as working hides, building houses out of willow, making tule duck decoys, constructing boats, and gathering and preparing pine nuts. Peg also taped four hundred hours of interviews with Wuzzie and Jimmie. In 1967, Peg put her collection of photographs and recorded conversations into a book, entitled *Survival Arts of the Primitive Paiutes*.

Jimmie George died on July 3, 1969, reportedly at age ninety-five. Several hundred people, including many former patients, attended the funeral, which was held five days later at the Fallon Indian Reservation. They came from California, Oregon, and all over northern Nevada to pay homage. The *Nevada State Journal* covered the event on July 20, 1969, noting that Wuzzie, her children, grandchildren, and great-grandchildren were all in attendance. Jimmie was buried in the Stillwater Tribal Cemetery.

After Jimmie's death, Wuzzie carried on their efforts to document and perpetuate the skills of the Paiute people. She worked with children in local schools and summer camps. She and Peg traveled to Pocatello, Idaho, where she constructed a cattail house as an exhibit in the Idaho State Museum. Several years later, she replicated the house for the Nevada Historical Society in Reno. Wuzzie also continued working with linguist Sven Liljeblad, with whom she and Jimmie had collaborated on recording the grammar and vocabulary of their language when Sven was at Idaho State University in the early 1950s. He moved to the University of Nevada, Reno in the 1970s, and he and Wuzzie resumed their efforts to save the language as well as cultural features—such as stories, myths, and legends—of the Paiute people.

Wuzzie suffered a stroke in 1976 and, after that, it became more difficult for her to speak and move. However, she helped produce the segments of the color film *Tule Technology: Northern Paiute Uses of Marsh Resources in Western Nevada*. Released in 1983, the film shows Wuzzie and other family members making a duck egg bag, cattail house, duck decoy, and tule boat. The forty-two-minute film is narrated by her son Leonard and granddaughter Lois. Catherine S. Fowler put the content into book format as part of the Smithsonian Folklife Studies in 1990.

In her final years, Wuzzie was cared for by granddaughter Louella Thomas. Winona had preceded Wuzzie in death, but her sons, Leonard, Ivan, Walter, and Ashley, often visited her with their families. She died in Fallon on December 20, 1983, according to the Nevada Death Index, quite possibly at the age of 100. A wooden cross with the name Wuzzie D. George stands over her grave in the Stillwater Tribal Cemetery.

The Churchill County Museum in Fallon has a permanent display of a tule home as well as other items made by Wuzzie and members of her family. Wheat's collection of interview tapes is housed in the Special Collections Department in the Getchell Library at the University of Nevada, Reno.

In 1995, the Nevada State Legislature commended Wuzzie and her family for preserving the traditions of the Northern Paiute of the Stillwater Marsh, as declared in Concurrent Resolution No. 30:

> RESOLVED BY THE ASSEMBLY OF THE STATE OF NEVADA, THE SENATE CONCURRING, That the members of the 68th session of the Nevada Legislature commend the Fallon Paiute-Shoshone Tribe and the George family for their efforts to honor and keep alive the memory of their ancestors by teaching their history and carrying on their work; and be it further RESOLVED, That the members of the Nevada Legislature commend Wuzzie and Jimmy George for their lifelong effort to develop and teach the traditions, crafts and skills of their ancestors.

Without Wuzzie's efforts (assisted by Jimmie) to preserve the traditions and skills of the Northern Paiute people, this knowledge would have been lost forever. Wuzzie created a legacy that lives on in books and films. Her family, the native community, and the general public have been enriched from her work as the guardian of her Paiute heritage.

6

ANNA FRANCES ELLESER RECHEL

(1884–1967)

Prospecting for Life and Country

Anna Rechel's family wanted her to leave Rawhide, a place surrounded by hills colored the various muted tones of brown often found in untanned leather. Anna had lived and prospected in this remote mining community—located halfway between Reno and Tonopah in Mineral County—for over thirty years. She loved desert life, but also realized she was getting older: "I don't think I'm any older than eighteen—it's just my body that's too old." Her worsening arthritis concerned her children. She hadn't told them about the day that she fell off the running board of her old battered truck while trying to start it. She had been badly bruised from that incident.

She also "forgot" to mention to her children some of the other dangers she had faced. She once shot a huge rattlesnake that slithered across her feet while she was resting in her living room. Another time, two long-haired men came to her house asking for water. Something about them bothered her, so she refused their request. Subsequent reporting on the presence of Charles Manson and his followers in the area suggests that her instincts were accurate, because the men were later convicted of multiple murders. She also never told her family about the people who shot at the purple bottles she had put on her roof in order to deepen their color. But she loved her home and

Anna Rechel, the last resident of Rawhide. —Courtesy of the Churchill County Museum & Archives, Fallon

refused to leave. After all, her nickname was "Rawhide Annie," and as a family member once noted: "She was probably about five foot two or three. But when she was strong-minded, you'd have thought she was six-feet tall."

Anna's house had been the social center of Rawhide. She once noted, "As for seeing people, I probably see more than I would in Fallon. In towns, everybody is too busy to visit." People stopped in to play chess or air their views. Anna was forthright with her opinions, especially about women's rights. She advocated for equal pay and for a woman's right to choose any profession that interested her— included prospecting. She fit right in with the women's liberation movement of the 1960s.

However, in that decade, Anna became the last resident in the town after Bill McGrath passed away. He was a big man with gentle manners, and Anna had enjoyed his company. He and Anna had dinner together every night and spent many hours reminiscing about their mining exploits around the area. One night, Bill died—or as it was called then, "skinned out"—while sitting in her rocking chair. It is reported that Anna buried him in the Rechel family plot in Hawthorne Cemetery, but cemetery records don't include his name. It would make sense that she did, however, because he was like family to her. Anna was suddenly alone in the desert.

•••

But her life didn't start that way. Anna Frances Elleser was a New Year's gift to her parents because she was born on January 1, 1884, in Pearl River, New Jersey—the youngest of seven children to John Christopher (anglicized from Johann Christoph) and Mary Huber Elleser. She enjoyed the lavish lifestyle her parents were able to provide. Anna grew up in a spacious mansion with a vine-covered veranda and glassed-in sunroom in Tappan, New York, about twelve miles north of New York City. Although she never learned much of the German language from her father's heritage, she embraced

German cooking, with sauerbraten a food she loved to prepare. According to the 1940 US Census, she left school after eighth grade, but she could do algebra and was an avid reader.

Reportedly a pretty girl, with auburn hair and a dimple in her chin, Anna married George Reed in 1904, but quickly realized the union was a mistake and began divorce proceedings. She was devastated when both of her parents died between 1905 and 1906, but she was later swept off her feet by the good looks and manners of another George, George F. Rechel, a local man who was also of German heritage. They married in 1911. However, divorce was uncommon at the time, and complications arose with her divorce from her first husband. The couple, Anna and the second George, headed to Nevada in 1912, which had a more lenient divorce process. Anna divorced her first husband again and remarried George Rechel.

Although accustomed to the lush greenery of New York, Anna discovered she liked the desert, so she, George, and her older brother Walter tried ranching at a site south of Fernley in Lyon County. Anna gave birth to six children over the next nine years, with four who survived: Rees (born in 1914); Fernley (1915); George, Jr. (1919); and Walter (1921), who was nicknamed "Pal." Life was not easy. They tried raising rabbits to sell in San Francisco, California, in addition to growing hay to sell to other ranchers. They also had to lease part of their land to a sheep rancher in order to stay afloat.

With money being so tight, Anna and her family would go prospecting for entertainment. When local miner Bill Stewart would drop by for an evening visit, Anna was enthralled by the stories of his mining adventures. Sitting by the wood stove, in the ranch kitchen illuminated by a Coleman lantern, he told tales of fortunes won and lost. She started reading everything she could find on the subject of mining and arranged family outings to the hills via hay wagon. While George was a casual rock hound, Anna was intense and looked at every outcrop carefully with a magnifying glass to see if it had value. Her daughter Rees later remarked, "She was in love with the hills." Prospecting allowed her to explore the world she could only glimpse from a distance at the ranch and also held the promise of a monetary reward.

Eventually, George and Walter worked in town. The 1920 US Census notes that George was working in a restaurant. Anna did the ranch work with the help of the children. The Great Depression, which started in 1929, was the final straw; they had to abandon the homestead. After briefly living in Fallon, the family moved to Rawhide in 1931. Life in such a small mining town was primitive, with no phone, fuel, or groceries. People learned to keep emergency gasoline in a five-gallon can that was ready if they had to leave town. Water was scarce and people saved rainwater as a backup to the water pipeline, which was completed in 1908 by the Rawhide Water and Power Company. Before that, residents bought what they needed from tankers that hauled it in, often on horse-drawn wagons, from Dead Horse Well about nine miles away. The going price for a barrel of water was $2.50, or five cents for a gallon.

From 1906 to 1907, Rawhide was a fast-growing gold camp, which the Mineral County Museum notes as having over "40 saloons, 30 hotels, 28 restaurants, 9 bakeries, 10 barbershops, 13 doctors, 4 hospitals . . . 9 lumberyards, and 125 brokerage offices." Three banks stayed open until midnight. Buildings were needed so quickly that an old lumber store from Wonder, Nevada, was moved to Rawhide and retained that name on the front of its wooden structure. Automobiles played a part in a mining boom for the first time; car stage lines ran from Fallon and other Mineral County towns such as Schurz and Mina (named for Ferminia Sarras, a famed female prospector known as the "Copper Queen"). At its peak in 1908, Rawhide's population soared to over seven thousand. Multiple newspapers, such as the *Rawhide Press-Times* and *Rawhide Rustler*, kept the busy population informed about local events.

Then good fortune turned. A fire started by an upset gasoline stove in the rooming house over the drugstore around nine o'clock

Panoramic photo of Rawhide, circa 1909. —Library of Congress, LC-USZ62-130239

on the morning of September 4, 1908, destroyed almost nine square blocks in the downtown business area. Many homes built entirely of wood burned, as well as tent structures. News of the blaze was wired to other places before the postal telegraph office burned. The headline of the *Reno Evening Gazette* on September 5th was "Rawhide Wiped Out." The article stated that three thousand people were left homeless, but the newspaper exaggerated the situation. Within two weeks, most structures were rebuilt with better materials.

A flood so large that it was heard five miles away dealt another blow to the town on August 31, 1909. This event was described in the *Colorado Springs Gazette* the following day: "The cloudburst occurred on the summit of the low hills to the north of the camp. In a few moments a three-foot wall of water was pouring down the slope, covering the three miles from the summit to Main Street with the speed of a railway train. The flood rushed into the street, which lies in a hollow and forms a general drainage canal, and every business house on the east side was flooded to a depth of from one to four feet." The title of the article, "Nevada Town Swept from Map by Cloudburst," was prophetic. The fate of the town was sealed. By late 1910, only five hundred people remained. When the Rechel party arrived in 1931, only about one hundred people still lived in Rawhide.

The Rechel family moved into a two-bedroom cabin that had once belonged to George Lewis "Tex" Rickard, a boxing promoter and the owner of the prosperous Northern Saloon in Goldfield in the early 1900s. Anna made the cabin homey with beloved quilts, antiques, and other items from their Fernley house. She spent her days prospecting, while George worked as an inspector for the state highway department. By working the tailings (waste rock) of old mines that boomed in the late 1800s, she found enough gold to buy food for her family at a time when many people couldn't support themselves. Anna thrived in this environment and dreamed of striking it rich. Her daughter Rees described her optimism: "She just knew that she was going to find it. It kept her going." Anna was the only female prospector in the Rawhide region.

Rawhide had no school, so Rees became the teacher of the younger boys until the state closed the one-room schoolhouse for having fewer than five pupils. After 1934, they went to Schurz for school. Schurz, named for Secretary of the Interior Carl Schurz (1877–1881), was located on the Walker River Indian Reservation. It was too far away for daily travel, so the children had to board with other families. While there, George Jr. experienced a burst appendix and had to come home to recuperate. Rees and Fernley both graduated from Churchill County High School in Fallon—in 1930

Anna checking out her finds. —Courtesy of the Churchill County Museum & Archives, Fallon

and 1932, respectively—and went on to the University of Nevada in Reno. Rees must have studied there for at least two years because she can be found in the 1931 and 1932 editions of *Artemisia,* the campus yearbook. She was a member of the Normal Club, a campus group for students who planned to become elementary school teachers. Fernley was also a Normal Club member in 1933 and 1934.

Misfortune struck the family twice in the years that followed. George had a stroke and could barely walk, even with a cane. George Jr. died on July 10, 1937, from peritonitis, an infection resulting from his burst appendix. On July 13, 1937, the *Nevada State Journal* described the situation as follows: "George RECHEL JR, seventeen years old, died at a local hospital Saturday afternoon (10 Jul 1937). An emergency operation for appendicitis had been performed on Friday morning. The youth was a resident of Rawhide where he had lived with his parents Mr. and Mrs. George (Anna) RECHEL SR for about four years, coming from Fernley (Nevada). . . . Funeral services were held Sunday afternoon in St. Phillip's church with Reverend D. B. NORTHRUP officiating. Interment was in the Hawthorne Cemetery."

His father, George Rechel, Sr., passed away six months later, on January 6, 1938, at age forty-three. He was also buried in the Hawthorne Cemetery. With her two daughters grown and gone (in 1933, Rees had married James Johannes Mortensen, a miner in Rawhide, and Fernley had married Henry Robert "Hank" Ketsdever on October 6, 1934), Anna had to provide for both her son Pal and her brother Walter, who had lost his money in a bank failure and seemed unable to cope with his situation. Walter was happy to have Anna handle most matters; even when she tried to get him to help with a chore, such as repairing a tire, she ended up doing it herself.

Rawhide was not doing well either. Only a few people remained, and the post office was officially closed on August 31, 1941. After that, all mail went to Fallon, which was located about fifty-five miles northwest of Rawhide in Churchill County.

With the onset of World War II, the US government banned the mining of gold so that miners would look for metals needed for the war effort. Anna mined tungsten, which was necessary in the manufacture of fifteen thousand different types of war paraphernalia. She now worked underground in hard hat and jeans, blasting away the dirt with dynamite. She filled buckets with the broken ore, which were lifted out with a winch from the twenty-five-foot shaft. Her brother helped her after Pal joined the Army in 1942.

Anna was heartbroken when she received word that Pal had been declared missing in action. He had been captured by the Germans in France and was held as a prisoner of war. Pal had married Helen LaRue Morgan before he left for Europe, so both she and his mother were happy to have him released in June 1945. As the *Reno Evening Gazette* reported: "Missing in Action since 28 Sep 1944,

Staff Sgt Walter E. RECHEL, sent a card to his mother, Mrs. A. (Anna) F. (Frances) RECHEL of Fallon Monday, stating he was a prisoner of war in Germany. Attached to the 4th armored division of the 3rd Army when reported Missing In Action, SGT RECHEL entered the service in 1942 after graduating from Churchill County High School."

Pal returned home, and he and his wife, who went by LaRue, settled down in Fallon. LaRue had grown up in Idaho near the Snake River, where plentiful irrigation water kept fields green, and thought Anna was crazy to choose to live in the bleakness of Rawhide, but said, "I got to know her, and know what she was doing. I got to admire her more all the time because I thought, 'This lady does what she wants to do. She goes ahead and does it. She doesn't listen to what other people tell her you ought to do.'" Anna taught LaRue to appreciate Nevada's mountains and desert lands.

The 1950s brought nuclear testing and atomic energy. Now Anna searched for uranium by walking the hills with a Geiger counter. She sought investors for her claims, but never acquired one. She drove an old pickup truck when prospecting, often sleeping on a mattress in the bed of the truck if too far away in the evening to get back to her cabin. She also found an old Spanish mine that had turquoise, which she polished and sold.

Anna happened to meet Alvin Nelson when the battery on her old truck died and he replaced it. Anna may have felt lonely, because her brother had died in February 1954, so when this old miner from Gabbs in Nye County proposed marriage and assured her he would buy her a new four-wheel drive truck, she accepted. Anna was seventy-two years old. But the marriage soured when he tried to get her to stop prospecting and just be a housewife who took care of him. She divorced Alvin. As her daughter Rees observed, "She wasn't about to be tied down."

When Anna's friend Bill McGrath died in the early 1960s, Anna became the sole resident of Rawhide. She viewed herself as the guardian of the town. She refused to let anyone, including members of her own family, remove anything from the historic buildings — even old boards. Tourists who might happen by found themselves invited in for tea by a woman with "a sharp-cut face with keen eyes, sparkling with humor," and Anna herself became somewhat of a tourist attraction. But she didn't always appreciate her visitors. As she told the *Indianapolis Star* in an article published on December 26, 1965: "I can't drive down to Schurz to do some shopping. When I get back, people might have taken some things from my house or I might find someone living there who just moved in without asking."

Although arthritis now bothered her, Anna still walked the hills looking for a promising strike. In the spring of 1960, however, she staked her last claim, which she named "Hope," demonstrating her never-ending optimism despite more than thirty years of hand-to-mouth prospecting. Pal and LaRue finally persuaded her to move to Fallon for her own protection in 1966. A newspaper reporter who visited Anna commented: "It is breaking her heart to pack up and move from the town she loves. One wonders if it might not be kinder to let her live out her days where she is so happy."

Anna returned to Rawhide whenever she could. One day, LaRue and Pal got a phone call in the middle of the night. Anna had suffered a heart attack. She died on August 21, 1967, and was buried at the Hawthorne Cemetery in Mineral County alongside her son and husband. Her grave is marked by a plain, flat stone inscribed with just her name and the dates of her life. The simple memorial is fitting for a woman who could have easily identified the type of stone used.

Today, nothing remains of Anna's beloved Rawhide. Vandals burned the town after she left. The original 1908 stone jail and cellar survived the fire, but the jail was later relocated to the city and county government complex in Hawthorne, where the building sits in front of the Mineral County Courthouse. The actual site of Rawhide was lost in the creation of a huge open-pit mine. Because of legal loopholes, Anna's family wasn't even paid for the land she owned and had paid taxes on for years. The mine stopped operating in 2003, and the area was designated as a landfill in 2006. Although the town of Rawhide has disappeared, some consider the site a ghost town.

Like many miners, Anna never made the big strike, but her efforts supported her family when the US economy collapsed. In the 1940 US Census, she listed her occupation as "prospecting." Over the years, mining allowed her to live life as she desired in the place she chose. Unlike many women in the state, she was passionate about the desert, despite the fact that the land around Rawhide has been described as "barren hills and sagebrush clumps." In a 1908 eulogy for Rawhide resident, Riley Grannan, it was noted that "in winter the shoulders of the mountains are wrapped in garments of ice and in the summer the blistering rays of the sun beat down upon the skeleton of the desert." Not many people would choose such a locale as their paradise, but Anna felt more like Idah Meacham Strobridge, known as "Nevada's first woman of letters," who wrote: "If you love the Desert, and live in it, and lie awake at night under its low-hanging stars, you know you are a part of the pulse-beat of the universe, and you feel the swing of the spheres through space. And you hear through the silence the voice of God speaking."

While female miners in Nevada were often referred to as "calico prospectors," naturalist John Muir's description of Nevada miners as a "race of giants" seems to more aptly embrace Anna's accomplishments. Besides contributing vital materials to the government for patriotic endeavors, Anna's monumental effort to care for her family and the town she adopted demonstrated true grit. Leaving the comforts of the East behind, she thoroughly embraced the rough-and-tumble lifestyle of the West and did whatever was needed to care for the people and place she loved.

7

THÉRÈSE ALPETCHE LAXALT
(1891–1978)

A Mother for the Basques of Nevada

Thérèse said *"Ongi etorri"* ("welcome" in Euskara, the Basque language) to the United States in 1920. Euskara is a complex language with various dialects and sprinkled with many x's, k's and z's. A cultural folktale states that the Devil tried to learn the language for seven years before giving up. Euskara is also very different from French and Spanish, which are spoken by the citizens of the two countries that surround the European Basque region in the foothills of the Pyrenees Mountains.

On September 24, 1923, Thérèse welcomed her second child into the world in a doctor's house in Alturas. This Spanish name, meaning "heights," aptly reflected the town's elevation of 4,370 feet in northern California. Her husband, whom Thérèse accompanied into this wilderness region, worked as a sheepherder and spoke some English. He was supposed to be her interpreter during the birth, but he ended up being caught and delayed in a violent snowstorm. Thérèse spoke no English and had no idea what the doctor was saying. Consequently, the child's birth certificate states "No Name Laxalt." The baby boy later became known as Robert Peter Laxalt, and he once commented about the situation of his birth: "Dad was caught in an early blizzard 40 or 50 miles out. Mother never forgave him."

Dominique and Thérèse Laxalt with their children: John, Robert, Peter, Marie, Paul, and Suzanne.
—Robert Laxalt Collection [UNRS-P1999-10-179], University Libraries, Special Collections Department, University of Nevada, Reno

Robert was one of the six children of Thérèse and her husband, Dominique, who were both Basque immigrants to the United States. The Basques are thought to be the oldest ethnic group in Europe, which they celebrate in the saying: "Before God was God and boulders were boulders, the Basques were already Basques." The Laxalts followed in the footsteps of many Basques who, beginning in the mid-1800s, were drawn to the American West. Although the lure of the California Gold Rush brought the early influx, later arrivals easily found work in the emerging livestock industries in California and Nevada. With their long history of tending sheep, the Basque men and boys were the preferred sheepherders of stockmen. It was a lonely life in the summer, when the sheep foraged on high mountains and the men were away from family and friends for months. In winter, the herders would bring their flock down to lower pastures and gather in towns such as Reno, Winnemucca, Elko, and Ely, where they stayed in "ostatuak"—Basque boardinghouses—like the one Thérèse and Dominique later ran in Carson City.

When Dominique returned to herding, Thérèse handled both the business of the boardinghouse and the children alone for many years at a time when most women lived in male-headed households and did not own their own businesses. Monique Laxalt, Robert's daughter, drew upon her grandparents' real life situation in her novel, *The Deep Blue Memory*: "She hired a girl to tend to the two baby boys, and for eighteen hours a day she cooked and cleaned and washed. The father [grandpa] would appear at intervals, tending bar until he became sick with cabin fever, then disappearing back into the hills."

On top of her already heavy workload, Thérèse assumed the role of second mother for the many Basques who stayed at their boarding-house, called the French Hotel. They felt at home there, especially the new, young arrivals from the old country. Over the years, her hotel would serve as a dating service, job agency, and assistance league. A sense of ethnic loyalty created strong ties among the Basques. Sheepherders wandering alone with their flocks may be the common stereotype of the Basque culture, but in reality, resilient women like Thérèse cultivated a close knit Basque community in Nevada. Is it any wonder that she would be recognized as the "Mother of the State of Nevada" for the care she provided her own children as well as many other Basques?

———•••———

Thérèse Alpetche was born on February 20, 1891, in the village of Saint-Étienne-de-Baïgorry in the French province of Basse Navarre (which means "Lower Navarre" in English). She was the daughter of

Jeanne Alpetche (born January 25, 1871) and a married man from Paris with whom Jeanne fell in love. Her mother must have decided to honor her French father, because her name uses the French spelling. In Basque, the spelling is "Terese" (meaning "harvester"—one who reaps). Thérèse's early life as a "child of the holy ghost," which is how illegitimate children were described, was difficult. Sometime in 1892 or 1893, Jeanne married Jean Bassus (who Thérèse called her uncle, never father) to whom Jeanne had been betrothed by her parents before she met her Parisian love. Although Jean Bassus had also been born in the Basque region of Basse Navarre in the village of Ahaxe around 1870, he had relocated to Bordeaux and became wealthy running the Hotel Amerika, which catered to Basques who were traveling to North and South America. He opted to move Jeanne to Buenos Aires in Argentina, a country that was a major emigration destination for many Basques in the nineteenth century. Thérèse was left in the care of her maternal grandparents in Baïgorry. While Jean and Jeanne were in Argentina, Thérèse acquired four Bassus half-siblings: brothers Jean Michel (1894) and Maurice (1895), and sisters Marie Claire (1902) and Aurélie (1904). When her family finally returned to France, they again settled in Bordeaux and continued to run the Hotel Amerika, as well as a travel agency, which was one of the first businesses to book trips for clients from Europe to America.

Thérèse developed an early interest in cooking fine cuisine, and she graduated from the renowned Le Cordon Bleu in Paris while in her early twenties. She temporarily returned to Bordeaux to care for her mother, who was fighting consumption, which we know today as tuberculosis. When an uncle cheated Thérèse out of her inheritance of their family home in Baïgorry, because of the circumstances surrounding her birth, she left the area for the last time and briefly returned to Bordeaux again. While there, her stepfather asked her to handle a family situation in America.

December 8, 1920, found Thérèse at age twenty-nine sailing from Bordeaux to New York City on the SS *Caroline*. She listed her final destination as San Francisco, California, because that was where she thought her half-brother Jean Michel was living and working as a farm laborer. He had served as a soldier in the French army during World War I and inhaled poisonous gas. Seeking treatment at the Letterman Army Hospital at the Presidio of San Francisco, he had traveled to the United States in October 1919. The doctor there sent him to Saint Mary's Hospital in Reno (Washoe County) where the climate was drier. Thérèse traveled to Reno, planning to take her brother home as her stepfather requested, but he was too sick to travel. Thérèse supported herself by working as a maid in the Indart (Basque) Hotel in Reno.

Here Thérèse met fellow Basque, Dominique Laxalt. He had been born July 14, 1887, in Laguinge-Restoue in the northern Basque province of Soule. He arrived in the United States in 1903 (although the 1930 US Census says 1904) and moved to Nevada around 1906. Dominique is described on his US World War I draft registration (1917–1918) as being a tall man with black hair and dark brown eyes, living in Lassen County, California, and claiming exemption because he was raising sheep for the war effort. By the 1920 US Census, he was living in Wichman in Lyon County, Nevada, and had applied for naturalization as a US citizen. Although he only attended school through the fourth grade, he spoke several languages and was an avid reader, always wanting new books and materials brought to him while he tended sheep.

Thérèse was charmed by Dominique—a dashing man who drove a Cadillac—and the couple married on October 8, 1921, at St. Thomas Aquinas Cathedral, which is still located on Second Street in Reno. Her brother died from pulmonary tuberculosis only a week later on October 14, 1921, and was buried at Mountain View Cemetery. Thérèse stayed in the United States with Dominique, thus becoming part of what is known as the Basque Diaspora, a group of people who had left their ancestral homeland.

Along with three partners, Dominique was one of the owners of the Allied Land & Livestock Company, a corporation with its original headquarters at a ranch in Fallon in Lyon County near Yerington, where the newly married couple lived. The offices had been relocated to the Odd Fellows Building in Reno on December 20, 1920. With around twenty thousand sheep and one thousand head of cattle ranging in Nevada and California, the company also grew a variety of crops on five ranches and farms. Thérèse thought she had found the perfect life in America, so opted at this time to drop the French spelling of her name and became Theresa. By the 1930 US Census, she was a naturalized US citizen and also decided to burn her French passport.

Disaster struck Dominique's business in 1922. The state's livestock market crashed and the loans the company had used to expand could not be repaid. The couple was broke. Dominique took the few sheep he had left to northern Washoe County to start over. A harsh winter took many of these livestock, too. To survive, the Laxalts moved around Nevada and northern California, where Dominique looked for work as a sheepherder and ranch hand. Their son Robert recalled their makeshift home in the Eastern Sierras in 1925: "I spent a couple years in Bodie, lived in a wooden shack with a dirt floor, when Papa was really bust." Whenever possible, Theresa put her Le Cordon Bleu cooking training to use as a ranch cook, often preparing meals for as many as thirty ranch workers. What she earned also helped them survive.

Theresa and Dominique started a family that eventually included six children: Paul (born 1922), Robert (1923), Suzanne (1925), John (1926), Marie (1928), and Peter (1931). In 1926, Theresa rebelled against the harsh, roving life, and the family settled in Carson City. Their frugality had allowed them to save the $100 needed as the down payment on the purchase of the French Hotel. Located on Carson Street, across from the Virginia & Truckee Railroad depot and close to the state capitol, the hotel was remembered by their son

Robert as a "little boardinghouse of four bedrooms, a dining room and a saloon." In reality, the 1870s two-story wooden building had four bedrooms upstairs, with one bathroom shared by all. The family lived downstairs in two bedrooms behind the dining room, kitchen, and bar. Their boarding clientele were mainly Basque sheepherders and railroad personnel.

Theresa was now able to prepare more elegant meals, incorporating the vegetables and chickens grown in their backyard. Her efforts attracted upscale guests to the dining room, including local politicians such as US Senator Patrick McCarran. He was much admired by the Basques because he championed their continued immigration while working to ban other ethnicities. The children helped in the restaurant, and their eldest child, Paul, became interested in politics by listening to the patrons.

Although Prohibition was the law of the land, they realized they had to serve alcoholic beverages to compete with other local establishments. Traditionally, wine is served with every course in Basque meals except dessert, where coffee is offered. Robert stated: "I suppose this made us bootleggers, but hardly in the league of Al Capone." Picon punch was a favorite, made by blending Amaro (a bitter Italian herbal liqueur), soda water, and grenadine together and pouring the mixture over ice in a glass with a lemon wedge garnish. A little brandy was floated on top as the final touch. This cocktail is still a staple of Basque restaurants and festivals, and the Nevada legislature has several times considered making it the official state drink.

Although Montpelier, Vermont, is currently the smallest capital of a US state, Carson City held that distinction from the 1920s up to the 1960s. Paul described his early life in the city in a 2008 interview published in *Nevada Magazine*: "We had a couple thousand people at best . . . . Only one street in Carson City was paved, and that was the main street. That was good because we not only didn't have much traffic, but Sundays were reserved for bike racing, which we would have from the front of the Capitol to our little [French] Hotel on Carson Street. We went to school in a building where we had all 12 grades, and our home was in walking distance of school and church."

But Dominique tired of this city life after a few years, and the lure of the mountains pulled him back to the sheep business. "As time passed, [my father] felt increasingly trapped," explained Paul. "Inside life simply wasn't for him." Dominique established herds in the mountains east of Carson City and near Dayton in Lyon County. Others he placed in the Washoe Valley between Reno and Carson City and at Marlette Lake, situated 8,200 feet above sea level, west of Carson City. Theresa continued to run their in-town business interests and raise the children alone. A gold-framed wedding picture and Dominique's suit from that day, which hung in the back of her bedroom closet, were her daily reminders of having a husband.

In 1931, Theresa decided to make a change. She leased the French Hotel to a Basque couple and bought the Ormsby House, a Carson City landmark at the corner of Second and Carson Streets. It had been built in 1859 by Major William Ormsby, a founder of the city, and opened early the following year. Although she operated it for a while as a boardinghouse, the building was in such disrepair that Theresa eventually decided to demolish the building and sold the land. Over the years, she tried various other businesses and gained a reputation as a shrewd businesswoman. The 1944 Carson City Directory shows her owning a liquor store. In 1972, Paul had the Ormsby House rebuilt three blocks from its original location. The grand ballroom was named the Crown Thérèse to honor his mother.

In 1935, Theresa paid $3,000 for a home at 402 North Minnesota Street, originally built in 1872 by Duane Leroy Bliss, also known as the "Lumber Baron of the Comstock Lode." Although the two-story, white-framed house had a living and dining room large enough for their family, it only had two bedrooms. To make it suitable, a large screened porch was added to the back of the house. In his 2000 memoir, Paul explained, "This became a dorm of sort for us four boys. Great in the summer, but a killer in the winter."

Theresa insisted that the children get a solid education and pushed them to learn English, so they never really learned the Basque language. She wanted them to be able to earn a living with their brains rather than with their hands. She bought them a typewriter on which to write their school papers, as well as boxing gloves for the boys so they could work out their own problems. One of the books in their house was an illustrated listing of every ranked prizefighter of that era, and the family gathered around the radio to listen to world championship matches. Robert exhibited such prowess as a boxer that he became a member of the Stewart Indian School Boxing Team—the only nonnative participant. Located southeast of Carson City, the purpose of this boarding school was to assimilate children from the various tribes into American culture. Although tasked with much work and responsibility, Theresa was intimately involved in the daily lives of the children. As Paul recalled, "In raising us, she ran a 'tight ship,' even oppressive by some modern day standards. When she made a family decision, that was it. No appeal. No due process."

When not at school, the Laxalt boys would join their father in his sheep camp. They loved being outdoors and eating sheepherder bread, a staple of Basque herders. They may have carved their initials or dates into the thin white bark of aspen trees, a habit of many lonely herders. Today we call these carvings *arborglyphs* and some are still visible in northern Nevada. William A. Douglass, an expert in Basque culture, explained their purpose as follows: "the Basque sheepherder humanizes an otherwise unrelentingly pristine natural environment . . . . despite his solitude a man can commune with the ghosts of past generations and enjoy some small sense of purpose as he leaves his own mark as a legacy for future herders."

But the boys did not care for the solitary work that their father relished. John, Peter, and Paul became attorneys. Bolstered by his interactions with politicians when he was a boy, Paul went on to politics and served as Nevada governor (1967–1971) and then two terms as US Senator for Nevada (1974–1987). Although Robert did use his hands for boxing, he also authored many books, articles, and stories, and in 1961 was the founding director of the University of Nevada Press. He was named the first Distinguished Nevada Author Chair at the University of Nevada, Reno. His sister, Suzanne, became Sister Mary Robert, a nun with the Holy Family Order, and Marie became a teacher.

Theresa's caring interactions with her children and others motivated the Leisure Hour Club of Carson City to nominate her to be their Mother of the Year in 1967. The Nevada Committee of the National American Mothers Organization agreed, and this led to Theresa's recognition as Mother of the State of Nevada for that same year. She was again recognized in 1976 as one of the twelve women named Nevada Mothers of Achievement in a national publication called *Mothers of Achievement in American History, 1776–1976*. In her nominating letter, Mrs. W. MacDonald Smith stated: "It is not often that one individual can be found who so well embodies the many traits of character which have come to be highly regarded in mothers; our nominee exemplifies to a rare degree the qualities of courage, cheerfulness, patience, affection, understanding, and homemaking ability."

Dominique retired from sheepherding in 1947, but after a visit to his Basque homeland in 1953, which became the basis for his son Robert's 1957 acclaimed book, *Sweet Promised Land*, he became restless again and returned to his beloved days as a herder. After a long illness, he died in Carson City in 1971, at age eighty-four. He was buried in Lone Mountain Cemetery. On his wooden grave marker are carved a sheepherder with one of his flock and the words, "His home was the hills."

At age eighty-seven, Theresa died on May 10, 1978, in San Jose, California, where she lived with her daughter, Sister Mary Robert. After a church service at St. Teresa of Avila Catholic Church in

Carson City, she was buried in the family plot in the Lone Mountain Cemetery. Although she had disavowed any personal connection to France since 1930, on her tombstone are the French words *Notre mère bien aimée*, which means, "Our beloved mother." She certainly was a loving mother for her own children as well as a surrogate mother for many other Basques for whom she provided a home away from home. At the time of her death, the *Nevada State Journal* published an article titled: "A Son's Tribute to His Mother" that was excerpted from Robert's book, *Sweet Promised Land*. It included:

> It took courage . . . for a woman to live in the sheepcamps. And it took courage not to keep on living that way, . . . with four children and a hundred dollars, to start another life in the little hotel, doing all the cooking for the workingmen boarders, on her feet from four o'clock in the morning until midnight. . . .
>
> Even after we left the hotel and my father had gone back to the hills . . . , it took courage to face a life with six children . . . , but it took something else, too . . . . It had to do with winter nights when the big trees outside the house moaned fearfully with blizzards, and long after the children had gone to bed, a single candle burned in the living room, and a wife prayed for her husband in the hills.

Today, Nevada students of Basque descent can apply for the Theresa Laxalt Scholarship at the University of Nevada, Reno. She would be pleased that her name is associated with personal advancement via education. This campus has the largest library and Basque studies center outside of the Basque country in France.

Reno is also home to the National Monument to the Basque Sheepherder, entitled "Solitude." Located in Rancho San Rafael Park, the twenty-two-foot-high bronze statue, erected in 1989, represents a sheepherder shouldering a lamb under the full moon. Those who want to experience the Basque culture firsthand can attend many Basque celebrations, including the National Basque Festival, held annually around the Fourth of July weekend in Elko. The date was specifically selected to celebrate the founding of the country that accepted Basque people like Theresa so readily. Today, Basque cake—a layered cake with an almond or vanilla custard filling, usually made around the holidays—has also been touted as the dessert that best represents Nevada.

There is a proverb that states: "Mother is a verb, not a noun." Theresa dedicated her life to both her immediate and extended Basque family in Nevada. She assisted the many young Basques who came to America because they had no opportunity to acquire family property in the old country (it always went to the oldest child). Whether through a business venture, such as the French Hotel, or cheering along with others when Basque children played sports at Carson High School, Theresa helped establish the Basques as an integral part of their adopted state. Even several generations later, the name Laxalt is prominent in Nevada, thanks to the achievements of Theresa, her children, and their offspring. It is only fitting that she be recognized for all the ways she contributed to her community and her state, and to her we say, *"Eskerrik asko"* ("thank you").

8

MARY HILL FULSTONE
(1892–1987)

Smith Valley Called Her "Doctor Mary"

Influenza, more often known as "the flu," is a viral infection that regularly causes severe illness in people. Its name comes from the Italian word meaning "influence," because it was originally thought that the illness was caused by the unfavorable influences of the stars and planets. Today, the belief that our lives are affected by celestial bodies is called astrology, and we know it has no actual bearing on people's health.

People who catch influenza usually get a high fever, a sore throat, and a headache. The illness also includes a runny nose, aching muscles, and coughing. Modern medicine has discovered that there are different types of flu, and treatment can be targeted for the specific variety. Although an annual flu shot can prevent—or at least minimize—the infection, many individuals in the United States still die from the flu each year. It is estimated that around twelve thousand Americans died during the 2015–2016 influenza season.

While that is a devastating loss of life, it seems small compared to what occurred in 1918 when Mary Hill was interning at the Children's Hospital in San Francisco, California. The flu that year infected five hundred million people globally and between fifty million and one hundred million of those died. It was known as the "Spanish Flu" because many people in that country were afflicted early and died. World War I still engulfed much of the world, and soldiers traveling back to the United States were thought to have brought the flu from Europe. The disease first appeared at Fort Riley, Kansas, and then spread throughout the country. In the United States, about 28 percent of the population became infected and over half a million people died.

The only treatments for Mary's patients were rest, the application of a mustard plaster, and inhaling steam. A mustard plaster, made by moistening powdered mustard seeds and putting them in a cloth, was

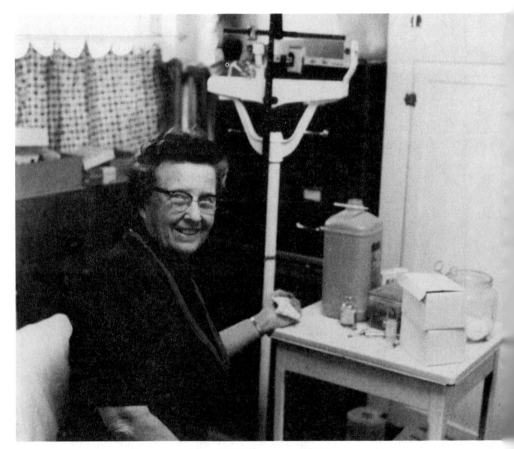

Mary Hill Fulstone, circa 1950.

applied to the chest to promote coughing and help clear the lungs. However, Mary had to watch the patient carefully, because a mustard plaster can burn the skin if left on too long. Mary rejoiced when a child recovered enough to spend time on the sunroof on the top of the hospital. She and the other medical staff worked long hours to keep the children alive. Unfortunately, not all of them recovered.

But Mary knew that laughter helped ease the intensity of the situation, and she had a lively sense of humor. One day she wondered aloud what she looked like under the mask she had to wear. This silly comment made everyone laugh. For a woman whose mother always feared Mary would get sick as a child—and often made Mary bypass a street with a house where someone was ill—becoming a doctor seemed an odd career choice. But along with humor, Mary brought many talents with her as she prepared to enter this male-dominated profession. A woman becoming a doctor in the early twentieth century was still frowned upon by society; only 5 percent of the practicing doctors in the United States were women. But Mary didn't care.

———•••———

Mary Ruth Hill was born in the small mining town of Eureka in north-central Nevada on August 3, 1892. Four years younger than her sister, Jennie, she was the second child of John H. and Ella E. Riley Hill. Her father, who had been an accountant for the Eureka & Palisade Railroad, now managed the store owned by Reinhold Sadler. Elected lieutenant governor of Nevada in 1895 and becoming governor in 1896 upon the death of Governor John E. Jones, Sadler offered John Hill the head commissary position at the Nevada State Prison. The family moved to Carson City for his job in 1896. Although Nevada had become a state in 1864 and the "city" was the state capital, its three thousand residents lived without indoor plumbing, running water, or electricity. They did enjoy summer concerts in the bandstand on the Capitol grounds.

Mary attended the one-room North Ward School, located at the edge of the town on West Telegraph Street, and then the imposing two-story Central School that sat at the corner of Minnesota and Telegraph Streets, close to the Capitol. She was a sociable girl and enjoyed playing games such as hide-and-seek and tag. She liked playing with Ida, Amelia, and Nellie, the daughters of Wilson Brougher, who had made a fortune during the silver strike at Tonopah in Nye County, bought the Arlington Hotel in Carson City in 1902, and was later elected as state senator from Ormsby County. The Hill family had begun living in that hotel in 1898 because it was closer to Central School. Although there was a large age gap between them, Mary was also friends with Belle Butler, the wife of Jim Butler, a miner who made a major silver strike in Tonopah in 1900 and started the rush that gave the town its reputation as the Queen of the Silver Camps. The Butlers' original claim is now part of the Tonopah Historic Mining Park.

Mary, who was a voracious reader, checked out as many books as she could carry from the school library. She would sometimes put a blanket over the window above her bedroom door so that she could read late into the night and her parents would not know she was still awake. Mary was athletic and enjoyed hiking, swimming, and camping. Between 1907 and 1911, when Mary was a student at Carson High School, she also liked to play basketball; she was captain of the girls' team that won the regional championship one year. Imagine having to run and shoot in heavy uniforms of "pleated, blue serge bloomers with long black stockings and a middy blouse." Although Mary described her childhood days as "most rigid, entirely under the control of the family, the church, and the school," she remembered being happy and busy.

Mary graduated from Carson High in 1911 in a class of eleven students. Her mother had trained to be a teacher at San Jose Normal School (now San Jose State University), so Mary was urged to become a math teacher because of her strong skills in that subject. She left

Nevada to attend the University of California, Berkeley. Mary enjoyed her math classes, but was quickly drawn to the sciences where she made friends with premed students. They encouraged her to switch her major, and she obtained a bachelor's degree in Biological Sciences in 1915. Mary went on to enroll in medical school at the University of California, San Francisco. One of just three women in the class of thirty-four students, Mary graduated near the top of her class in 1918. She completed a residency at San Francisco County Hospital and then moved to the Children's Hospital just in time for the flu epidemic. Afflicted children would be brought to the hospital by their mothers in the morning and die by nightfall. Mary always recalled those days as "a dreadful time."

While visiting her sister, who was teaching in Smith Valley in Lyon County, Mary met tall, blue-eyed Fred Moline Fulstone. He had been born to a Nevada pioneer family in Genoa on May 4, 1889. According to the 1940 US Census, Fred had only attended school through the sixth grade, a common situation for kids who worked on ranches and farms in the rural west at the turn of the century. The pair hit it off and Fred and Mary married on July 16, 1919, in Reno. Mary still needed to finish her residency in internal medicine, so she returned to St. Francisco County Hospital. In 1920, Mary completed her studies and took the Hippocratic Oath, which states the obligations and conduct standards for doctors. Her license was listed annually in the *California, Occupational Licenses, Registers, and Directories, 1876 to 1969*.

Mary and Fred returned to Smith Valley to their home on his six-hundred-acre ranch where she opened her medical practice and he raised hay, cattle, and sheep. The house, originally built in 1879, had been expanded to eight rooms and the young couple quickly filled it with children. Fred Jr. was born at the ranch in 1920. Over the next nine years, four more children followed, all delivered at the Children's Hospital in San Francisco by one of Mary's favorite instructors in the doctor training program, Dr. Elizabeth Keyes. The children included David Hill, who was born in 1923, followed by Richard Nelson in 1927, and twin girls, Eleanor and Jeanne, in 1929.

Mary quickly became known as "Doctor Mary" rather than "Dr. Fulstone." Before she arrived in the Smith Valley, the nearest doctor was twenty-five miles away, in Yerington. While there may have been some who frowned upon medical treatment provided by a woman, Mary didn't recall it that way. Referring to how she was accepted as a doctor, she stated in her oral history: "On the whole, I think the people in Smith Valley started right in and came here." The Paiutes who worked on their ranch were also her patients. The Indian Agency offered her $90 per month to care for all the Paiutes in the area, and Mary traveled many miles out of Smith Valley to see these patients. As she got to know the Paiutes, she became comfortable leaving her household and children in the care of Paiute housekeepers and babysitters, if needed, while she was away on medical calls. Mary's mother also often cared for the "Fulstone five," as the children were known.

The main focus of Mary's practice was pregnancy, birth, and children. It is believed that she delivered more than four thousand babies over the course of her career. But she did deal with other medical needs when they arose. One time a man was badly hurt after his wagon turned over, with a broken knee, a broken ankle, and a dislocated shoulder. As a slight woman who was a little over five feet tall, Mary did not have the strength to reset his shoulder. However, she figured out what was needed and directed Fred, who did the physical pulling. Mary often recruited fathers to help during the delivery process because in many rural settings no one else was available. She did not have a phone or electricity in her home. She was one of the few people in the Smith Valley to own a car, but the roads were sometimes impassable, such as in the winter of 1933 to 1934 when the snow was as tall as the fence posts. Mary's son David would drain the water from the car every night so that it wouldn't freeze, expand, and crack the radiator. Mary sometimes used a horse and buggy to get to where she was needed.

Mary charged for her services according to what a family could afford. Her normal fee to deliver a baby was $35 (about $435 in 2018). During the Depression years (1929 to 1939), people had little money, and Mary often did not send a bill. Sometimes she was paid with livestock or farm products that helped feed her family. Once she was given a pig, and Fred cared for it while trying to find a buyer. Months later, he sold the pig for $360, but it had cost him $362 to care for it, so there was no profit in that deal. Mary always provided care and treatment, regardless of her patients' ability to pay. Sometimes, her medical skills were expanded beyond the norm; young girls in the area asked her to pierce their ears.

In 1938, Mary expanded her practice to Yerington three days each week to help out the lone doctor. She would do her morning office hours in Smith Valley and head to Yerington in the afternoon. Mary knew it would take a better hospital to draw medical professionals into the area, so she started a campaign to get a new facility built in Yerington. In 1953, the voters of Lyon County passed the bond issue that funded the construction of the Lyon Health Center, completed on March 24, 1954. Three major and four minor surgeries were performed there that day. No longer did people have to go to Reno for every medical procedure. One wing was named the "Doctor Mary" in Mary's honor on March 24, 1963. The dedication plaque states:

> In recognition of her many years of selfless devotion to the people of this community and to her inspiring leadership toward achieving and maintaining the high standard of patient care.

In the 1970s, Mary served as chief of staff for the hospital, adding administrative duties to her already busy schedule.

Mary's early goal of becoming a math teacher, coupled with having five children, must have led to her strong interest in education. She was elected to the local school board and was instrumental in getting the small schools to join together to become the Smith Valley Consolidated School District. She served on its board for twenty-four years. The year she served as board president, she handed out diplomas to the graduating students and realized she had delivered all of them as babies. Mary became a member of the Nevada State Board of Education in 1957 and served until December 31, 1976.

While Mary maintained an active professional life in state and county medical societies, she also loved to play bridge and host parties. The annual hospital staff meetings in November included a pheasant hunt followed by a Thanksgiving-style dinner on the Fulstone ranch. She belonged to Soroptimist International, Delta Kappa Gamma (a teachers' organization), the American Association of University Women, Beta Sigma Phi (an international women's friendship network), and Order of the Eastern Star (associated with the Freemasons).

Her family enjoyed doing things together, and many days ended around the baby grand piano Mary bought with money earned from her practice. They could sing as loudly as they wanted because they had no close neighbors who would complain. Vacations were limited, as Mary once noted: "Every time I start to go away, the phone rings and a baby is about to be born." But Mary and her family did enjoy time at their summer cabin near Lake Tahoe, about fifty-five miles from Smith Valley. Purchased in the 1930s, the place near Round Hill on Marla Bay became their retreat. It was here that a woman once asked her daughters, who were playing on the beach, if their mother *practiced* medicine. One quickly responded, "Oh, no, she knows how."

Mary was proud that her twin daughters, when they were juniors at the University of Nevada, were selected out of over two thousand sets of twins to be the "Toni Twins" in 1950. The Toni Company produced hair permanents, a kit that contained materials to curl the hair that could be applied by the consumer at home. They promoted their product through ads showing twin girls with identical hairstyles and asked, "Which twin has the Toni?" Along with the national title, the girls received a month-long trip to Europe. Fred and Mary flew with them from New York City on June 19, 1950, and accompanied them as they visited England, Sweden, Belgium, Holland, Italy, and France. The passenger lists of the RMS *Queen Mary* show them sailing back to New York City from France in August 1950.

Mary received many honors throughout her career. In 1950, she was named Nevada's Mother of the Year and Delta Zeta Sorority's Woman of the Year. She had joined this group at the University of California, Berkeley. The Nevada Medical Association named her Nevada's Doctor of the Year in 1961 and the University of Nevada designated her as a Distinguished Nevadan in 1964. On April 8, 1976, the US Congress passed a *Congressional Record* tribute placed by Nevada Senator Paul Laxalt in her honor. It states in part: "It requires a special kind of person to dedicate himself to a life of looking after the sick and injured in a setting which means long hours and little monetary reward when compared to urban practitioners. Lyon County is fortunate enough to have such an individual in Dr. Mary Fulstone. She has been working . . . full throttle, commuting at all hours, often under very arduous conditions, to care for her patients."

In 1979, Mary and Fred served as the grand marshals of the Nevada Day Parade in Carson City. In 1984, the Nevada Women's Fund recognized Mary's "community involvement and significant community contributions" by inducting her into their Hall of Fame. However, one event was the most special for Mary. At the age of eighty-eight, she delivered her great-granddaughter, Kimber Lee.

At age ninety-one, after more than sixty years as a practicing physician, Mary retired. She was not ready to quit, but glaucoma stripped enough of her vision that she had to stop. Mary garnered the distinction of being the longest-practicing physician in Nevada. Some people still sought her advice and care after her formal retirement.

Fred and Mary celebrated their fiftieth wedding anniversary in July 1969. They shared the day with the US astronauts landing on the moon. As Mary later noted in an oral interview: "I just sometimes think how lucky I am that I had such a good husband. I don't suppose I'd ever been able to [have a medical practice] like I did if I had a different type of husband." But Fred had never been a good patient for Mary when he got sick. Once Mary had to threaten him: "Fred, if you don't get in this house I'm going to throw rocks at your cows." After a brief illness, Fred died on January 8, 1985. The couple had spent almost sixty-six years together.

After suffering a stroke, Mary died on December 2, 1987. In order to accommodate the large number of attendees, her funeral service was held in the Smith Valley High School gymnasium. Mary and Fred are buried next to each other in the Hillcrest Cemetery in Smith Valley. His tombstone has a lamb on it—a tribute to his life as a rancher. Hers has a caduceus (two snakes entwined around a staff with wings), which is used in the United States as a symbol of medicine. Mary's son David recalled two pieces of advice shared by his mother: "only hard work brought a person a rewarding life" and "don't wait until retirement to enjoy life. Savor each day."

In the 1990s and early 2000s, the Fulstone ranch operated as the Smith Valley Bed and Breakfast. Guests got to see where Mary practiced medicine and the many outbuildings Fred used on the ranch. Visitors to the Lyon County Museum can now see a recreation of Mary's medical office in its exhibits.

Fred and Mary's influence continues today. The Fulstones were early supporters of the University of Nevada, Reno (UNR), and Mary was a mentor to students after the medical college opened there in 1969. Students can still be assisted by the Dr. Mary Fulstone Endowment for Excellence Fund at the University of Nevada, Reno School of Medicine. Others from outside the medical field can benefit from the Richard Fulstone Family Scholarship administered by the UNR Foundation.

Dr. Mary became a doctor when medical knowledge was still limited. The antibiotics routinely given today were unknown, and many people died from illnesses that are now easily treated with modern drugs. Mary originally had to rely on morphine, chloroform, and aspirin to relieve pain, and she sterilized her instruments and other items—such as linens and basins—in the oven to make them sanitary. She applauded and publicly touted the advances in medicine during her lifetime.

Mary never saw herself as a feminist. As she once told a newspaper reporter, "I just never have associated myself with the women's lib movement . . . . If you're busy, you're not restricted because of your sex in the practice of medicine." When asked if she wouldn't have rather practiced specialized medicine in an urban setting, Mary countered that there was a place for general practitioners and country doctors like her: "There is something special and fulfilling about being a rural doctor. It's the people who make it so. It's like being part of each family." Mary, during her medical residency, had actually turned down an offer that would have appointed her to the prestigious Mayo Clinic based in Rochester, Minnesota. Mary relished being the rural doctor who loved her patients and was beloved by them.

9

ALICE LUCRETIA SMITH
(1902–1990)

BERTHA WOODARD
(1916–1999)

A Mighty Civil Rights Duo

While Las Vegas embraces the label of "Sin City" in the twenty-first century, Reno garnered that title for much of the early twentieth century. Its perceived scandalous reputation started in 1906 with the highly publicized divorce of Laura Corey, whose husband, William, was then president of US Steel, a large industrial corporation based in Pennsylvania. She charged him with desertion and requested custody of their sixteen-year-old son, Allan. An alimony settlement had been arranged through their lawyers. Mrs. Corey came to Nevada because the six-month residency period—required at the time to obtain a divorce—was more lenient than in other states. Nevada also allowed seven possible reasons for the divorce request. These included nonsupport, drunkenness, imprisonment, adultery, desertion, impotence, and extreme cruelty. "No fault divorce" was not allowed anywhere in the United States until 1970. Mrs. Corey was granted her requests and received a settlement of $3 million (which would be about $80 million today).

Other women took notice as newspapers throughout the country covered the event. By 1909, Reno had become the country's "new divorce headquarters," and people (records show 60 percent were women) flocked there to sever marital ties. When the Great Depression hit in 1929, the Nevada legislature again looked at divorce as a way to keep the state economy stable. In 1931, they reduced the residency requirement for divorce from three months to six weeks. It is no wonder that of the almost twenty thousand permanent residents of Reno at the time, around one hundred of them were divorce lawyers. During the 1930s, the Washoe County Courthouse processed more than thirty thousand divorce cases. Walter Winchell, a famous newspaperman and gossip columnist of that era, quipped that the change that depressed spouses went through during their six-week stay in the Silver State was "Reno-vation."

Women often celebrated their new freedom by kissing the columns at the entrance to the Washoe County Courthouse, as evidenced by Alfred Eisenstaedt's famous photograph that appeared on the cover of *Life* magazine on June 21, 1937. The long-told story of the newly divorced tossing their wedding rings into the Truckee River from the Virginia Street Bridge (called the "Bridge of Sighs") was thought to be a legend until prospectors with a dredge started pulling up rings from the river bottom in 1976. "I'm on my Way to Reno" was a popular song sung by Billy Murray and sold on an Edison Standard Record in 1910. From 1910 to 1985, more than sixty major motion pictures incorporated the Reno divorce theme into their plots.

Gambling further enhanced Nevada's appeal when it was legalized in March 1931. When Prohibition, which banned the sale of alcoholic beverages, was repealed in 1933, Reno became an even greater draw for many people. Newspaper articles promoted Reno's hotels (especially the seven-story El Cortez, the tallest building in the city) along with plentiful residential accommodations around the area such as the Pyramid Lake Ranch, known as "Nevada's largest and most popular dude ranch." An article in the April 1934 edition of *Fortune Magazine* described the town as follows: "Reno lies in Nevada's western corner, ten miles from California. Population 18,500. Elevation 4,500 feet. Reputation: bad."

All of this activity created job opportunities in Reno, but the city was not as welcoming to African Americans as it was to whites seeking divorce, gambling, and fun. Reno openly practiced racial segregation, although there were no legal mandates to do so as there were in the South, which had restrictive Jim Crow laws (statutes named after a black character in minstrel shows in the 1800s). Some businesses were blatant about their prejudice. A sign in the window of a Fourth Street restaurant warned, "No Indians, dogs or Negroes Allowed." A downtown club advertised, "Colored Trade Not Solicited." Many other shops had similar signage.

The Ku Klux Klan (KKK) was active in the state, although it focused on developing small, local units called klaverns rather than a statewide organization due to the scattered population. Reno residents became aware of the KKK on April 5, 1924, when a burning cross lit up the sky in the city. The *Nevada State Journal* on October 18, 1924, reported the success of their recruiting efforts: "One hundred and thirty-four white-robed klansmen . . . solemnly and slowly walked two by two last night in the first public demonstration of the Ku Klux Klan in Reno . . . . Every street corner was packed solidly with spectators . . . . In front of the long procession was carried the American flag."

Many Reno residents shared these racial prejudices, which also included resentment toward the Asian population that had remained in the area after the mining booms of the late 1800s. In addition, several "sundown towns" in the Carson Valley reportedly blew a whistle each day at six p.m. to warn Indians to leave. Despite the racial prejudice in northern Nevada, African Americans Alice Lucretia Smith and her husband, Alfred, moved to Reno in 1938; in 1949, employment as a nurse brought Bertha Woodard there. Alice

Smith and Bertha Woodard faced the discrimination problem head on, making life better for all minorities.

———•••———

A descendent of slaves, Alice Lucretia Smith was born on November 4, 1904, in Bay St. Louis, Mississippi, the oldest child of John and Virginia Smith. Life was hard, but deep religious faith helped her and her siblings overlook their poverty. Encouraged by her mother to get an education, Alice graduated from the public school system and decided to become a teacher. She earned a teaching credential from Mississippi State Normal School in Hattiesburg in three years. Alice taught in the rural Mississippi towns of Waveland and Kiln, receiving a salary of $30 per month. Out of this, she had to pay room, board, and transportation costs.

To increase her income, Alice also worked for a while at Gulfside Assembly, a sixty-acre segregated black resort in Waveland. When it opened on January 24, 1924, it was the first facility on the entire Gulf Coast where African Americans were allowed to swim and enjoy the beach. It included a twenty-two-bedroom mansion that reportedly had housed a nephew of President Andrew Jackson. In 1968, when black and white Methodists joined together to form the United Methodist Church, this mansion became the meetinghouse for the activities of the integrated congregation, whose members enjoyed this retreat together despite the strict racial segregation laws in Mississippi. Alice probably taught at the Poor Boys' School, where underprivileged African American boys from all over Mississippi could receive a public school education. Today, the location is recognized by the State of Mississippi as a historic site and is being rebuilt in the wake of Hurricane Katrina, which demolished every building in 2005.

Alice decided to continue her own education and entered Alcorn College, an institution created by the state in 1871 to educate the descendents of slaves. It is the oldest black land-grant institution in

Alice Lucretia Smith. —Alice L. Smith Photograph Collection, University Libraries, Special
Collections Department [UNRS-P1993-08-01], University of Nevada, Reno

the United States. However, she only attended for one year before she dropped out and got married.

Alice liked having Smith as her last name. She once commented that she had the opportunity to marry other men named Smith, but Alfred "Al" Oscar Smith won her heart. Although he was born on June 14, 1893, in Ocean Springs, about thirty miles from where she was born, they did not meet in Mississippi. Like many other Southerners who saw opportunity in California, both went there seeking jobs. They met in Oakland and married in 1935. Deciding that prospects were better in Nevada, they moved to Reno in 1938 and both worked several jobs to survive. Despite her credentials and teaching experience, Alice took the only jobs offered to black women in the Reno-Sparks area at that time—as a maid and nanny. At one point, she and Al worked for the local Joseph Magnin department store.

Al had served in the army during World War I. When he tried to use the services of the Veterans Administration Hospital in Reno, he was denied care several times due to his race. Seeing and experiencing blatant racism led Al and Alice to establish the first Nevada chapter of the National Association for the Advancement of Colored People (NAACP) in 1944. Only a few other people met with them that day in their living room. Al was elected to serve as the president from 1944 to 1945, and Alice became the secretary of the Reno-Sparks branch. Alice remarked, "And, I felt that if you want to assume the responsibility of leadership, that you will just join the group trying to go forward. I do not think that the problem is any different to the minority leaders—that poor, old, over-worked word "minority"—and I do hope and trust that one day we will be able to eliminate that and just join forces and go forward in whatever is for the betterment of communities."

To obtain the fifty people needed for a charter, Alice and Al went door-to-door to solicit members. Many of the names on the charter application submitted to the NAACP used the address 226 Bell Street, a boardinghouse with black occupants near the Bethel African

Methodist Episcopal (AME) Church. Built in 1910 and called the "Biggest Little Church in the West," it is the oldest continuing African American church in the state and is on the National Register of Historic Places. After the first organizational meeting, the executive meetings of NAACP Reno-Sparks Branch No. 1112 were often held at that church.

Alice and Al also worked together to start the Robert H. Brooks Post of the American Legion because African American veterans were not allowed in other posts in Reno. Named for a black soldier killed in December 1941, and posthumously honored, this organization helped other veterans but was too late to help Al. He died on December 14, 1946, probably because he was denied care initially. He is buried at the Golden Gate National Cemetery in San Bruno, California, which was dedicated on May 30, 1942, as a final resting place for veterans.

But Alice would not allow herself to be bitter. As she told a newspaper reporter in a 1978 interview, she decided to "do something constructive" rather than "wasting time with that foolishness." She dedicated her life to helping her fellow man. She once commented: "We're all human beings despite the color of our skin, and I'm concerned about people in general, regardless to the color of their skin." When asked what she would prefer to be called as far as race (Negro, black, or African American), she would reply, "Please refer to me as an American."

Alice became what she called "busier than a cranberry merchant." Besides her work with the local NAACP chapter (she was president from 1955 to 1957), she was an active member in the Nevada League of Women Voters (which she helped charter); the American Red Cross; the Washoe County Council of United Church Women; the Sparks Business and Professional Women's Club; Reno's Economic Opportunity Board (now called Community Services Agency); the South Gate Chapter Order of Eastern Star (associated with the Freemasons); the Bethel AME Church; and the Sparks United Methodist Church, which she joined in 1961.

Governor Mike O'Callaghan appointed Alice as a delegate to the 1971 White House Conference on Aging due to her participation on the Advisory Committee of the Nevada Division of Aging Services and the Nevada State Welfare Board. In 1972, Alice received the Service to Mankind Award from the Sierra Nevada District of Sertoma International, a group of service clubs that are still active today and focus on hearing issues.

Alice was chosen to represent the state at a United Nations conference in San Francisco in 1974. The following year, she was honored in *Who's Who Among Black Americans*. That same year, the Sparks Business and Professional Women's Club chose her as their Woman of the Year. Beginning in 1976, the Alice Smith Award, established by Reno's Community Services Agency, was presented to the board member who had contributed the most to the community during the previous year. Alice had served as chairperson of this board for two years after its beginning in 1965.

Alice stayed true to her goal. She spent almost fifty years working for equality before medical problems confined her to a local convalescent hospital. She died in Reno on August 6, 1990, one year after Alice Smith Elementary School, in Golden Valley, north of Reno, was named in her honor. Her portrait is painted on a wall at the school, a reminder of her dedication to education. Alice once noted, "I am vitally concerned about our young people. . . . They are too young to realize that attempting to go their own way just isn't the right way . . . education is needed." Alice is buried near Al in the Golden Gate National Cemetery.

Alice, through her tireless efforts, made great strides for civil rights and tolerance in Reno. "Let's not throw away our lives," she once said. "Let's do something constructive. I always feel like I want to climb up a little bit, and maybe I can take someone with me." As it turns out, she did. Standing right beside her for a while and later continuing Alice's work in this endeavor was Bertha Woodard.

———•••———

Born on January 25, 1916, Bertha Rosanna Sanford grew up in Pasadena, California. Her parents, Samuel and Lillie Belle Menefield Sanford, had four children in Florida before moving to California and having two more. Joseph, Endora, Edward, and Korutte were born in Florida. Bertha and Lorenzo were born in California. The 1910 US Census reports the family living in Pasadena, so they must have moved there sometime after Edward was born in 1908.

Charles Cowen, Mayor Pro Tem, Reno; Bertha Woodard, NAACP Branch Secretary; Mrs. Grant Sawyer, wife of Governor Sawyer; Nathaniel S. Colley, Sacramento, NAACP guest speaker.
—University Libraries, Special Collection [UNRS-P1997-56-0417], University of Nevada, Reno

Bertha's interest in racial equality started while she attended John Muir High School. A member of the Girls' Athletic Association, she protested against the city's segregated swimming pools. After graduation, she went on to Pasadena City College. An interest in the medical field took her to Washoe Western School of Practical Nursing in Reno in 1949. Students completed a forty-eight-week course of study that made them eligible to take the Nevada nursing board licensed practical nurse examination. Bertha then worked at the Washoe Medical Center, later becoming the first African American on the Nevada State Board of Nursing (1967–1975).

Bertha married Ulysses Simpson "Woody" Woodard, who was born on May 22, 1902, in Gregg County, Texas. In 1932 he came to Nevada, where his training as a machinist helped him get one of the coveted jobs building Boulder (now Hoover) Dam on the Colorado River near Las Vegas. After its completion, he held various positions with the Greyhound Bus Lines in Reno until 1969.

Like Alice and Al, Bertha and Woody were appalled at the levels of segregation and prejudice throughout the city. Before it burned in 1962, the barbershop in the Golden Hotel would only cut a black man's hair after dark with the shades on the windows drawn. They too had seen the discriminatory signs in the windows of the stores and restaurants.

When a member of the black community got in trouble with the law, Bertha and Woody worked tirelessly on that person's behalf. Bertha led sit-ins and stood on picket lines promoting equal rights for African Americans. Also a member of the Reno-Sparks Chapter of the NAACP, she served as president from 1971 to 1976 and again from 1987 to 1988. Woody held that position before her, from 1969 to 1970. Both were involved in that organization on the state and national level as well. The *Reno Evening Gazette* reported on January 16, 1969, that what Bertha and Woody hoped to achieve for their community included "more minority group teachers, more counselors in schools, more job opportunities."

When black entertainers such as Sammy Davis Jr. and Louis Armstrong performed in Reno, they were not allowed to stay in the hotels where they entertained. Bertha made sure they had a place to sleep. She worked to get the Reno fire department as well as the churches integrated. Bertha was the only black member of the congregation of the United Methodist Church (now First United Methodist Church of Reno) and, like Alice, attended services at the Sparks United Methodist Church for many years.

Bertha knew that the world would scrutinize the entire Reno area when the 1960 Winter Olympics came to Squaw Valley. Prior to that event, she tried unsuccessfully to get the Reno City Council to lift its ban on minorities in local casinos and remove the bigoted signs that had bothered her and Alice. Bertha organized picket lines in front of the Overland Hotel and Harold's Club (both now gone), pushing for equal access for African Americans, who were not permitted as customers. This tactic had been successful in Hawthorne in Mineral County, where blacks protested against that town's only restaurant— located inside the El Capitan Casino—which denied service to people of color.

Finally, in 1961, Nevada passed its first civil rights bill. Governor Grant Sawyer invited Bertha to watch him sign it. The bill established the Nevada Commission on Equal Rights of Citizens (now known as the Nevada Equal Rights Commission). It became state policy as outlined in the Nevada Revised Statutes to "protect the welfare, prosperity, health, and peace of all people of the state . . . without discrimination or restriction because of race, religious creed, color, age, sex, disability, sexual orientation, gender identity or expression, national origin or ancestry" (NRS 233.010; 1).

Woody died on March 26, 1973, and was buried in Mountain View Cemetery. An editorial about him in the *Nevada Evening Gazette* two days later stated: "People everywhere learned to look up to him as a counselor, full of wisdom and as a gentleman. Such men are few, and when they are gone, they leave a large void." Just as Alice had

Bertha S. Woodard and Alice Smith (center back) at a civil rights meeting with Governor Grant Sawyer, Carson City, in January 1961. —Nevada Black History Project, University Libraries, Special Collections Department [UNRS-P1997-56-0326], University of Nevada, Reno

done when she lost her husband, Bertha continued with her efforts for racial equality after losing Woody.

In 1981, Bertha was honored for her outstanding service to the state with the Distinguished Nevadan Award, the most prestigious award conferred by the Board of Regents of the Nevada System of Higher Education. She was also pleased when President Ronald Reagan signed the bill on November 2, 1983, that made Martin Luther King, Jr.'s birthday a national holiday.

In order to construct a record of the history of the civil rights movement in Nevada, Bertha started working with a group of students at the University of Nevada, Reno in 1999. She did not live to see it finished. Bertha died on September 16, 1999, at the Washoe

Medical Center, where she had worked for over seventeen years. She was buried at Mountain View Cemetery. Lonnie Feemster, president of the Reno-Sparks chapter of the NAACP from 1999 to 2002 and a long time resident of Reno, lamented: "Aside from her great enthusiasm, the biggest loss to this community is she had so much knowledge and first-hand experience of what happened here. Even though there are bits and pieces of what went on, we don't have a personal rendition of civil rights in Nevada."

On April 3, 2001, the Nevada State Legislature honored her passing with a resolution that recognized her efforts to break down racial barriers in the state. Senate Concurrent Resolution No. 27 praised her strength and enthusiasm for this cause. Due to her long association with the NAACP, the Woodard family presented her papers to that organization for safekeeping.

Alice and Bertha spent much of their lives in Nevada fighting prejudice and raising the public consciousness about racism. Although both always remained ladylike in appearance and manner, they actively confronted the barriers that African Americans faced in Nevada through their work with the NAACP and many other organizations. As two strong and opinionated women, they did butt heads at times about the leadership of the local NAACP chapter, as reported by the *Nevada State Journal* in 1974. But a common goal united them and kept them working together.

If one person can make a difference, look what these two did together to help Nevada shed its negative label as the "Mississippi of the West." By changing the attitudes of the residents in Reno, "The Biggest Little City in the World," as it is now known, Alice and Bertha expanded the interpretation of that label to embrace inclusiveness. The lives of all Nevadans were enriched because of their unwavering efforts.

10

LILLY ONG HING FONG
(1925–2002)

Higher Education Knows Her Well

Life was challenging if you were Chinese in the western United States at the end of the nineteenth century. In 1879, President Rutherford B. Hayes stated that the "present Chinese invasion . . . should be discouraged . . . . I would consider with favor any suitable measures to discourage the Chinese from coming to our shores." Prejudice was even exhibited in literary works from prominent writers like Bret Harte. Known best for his stories about the California Gold Rush, his 1870 poem "The Heathen Chinee" and Henry Grimm's four-act play "The Chinese Must Go," published in 1879, reinforced the anti-Chinese sentiment appearing in the United States. Negative feelings continued and deepened, resulting in the Chinese Exclusion Act, which was passed by Congress and signed into law by President Chester A. Arthur on March 6, 1882. This legislation provided a ten-year moratorium on Chinese labor immigration, although some exceptions were made for ministers, diplomats, teachers, students, merchants, and those just traveling through the country. In 1888, the law was broadened to exclude "all persons of the Chinese race." The Chinese already in the United States were prohibited from becoming citizens.

When the Chinese Exclusion Act expired in 1892, Congress extended it for another ten years through the Geary Act. This law forced each Chinese resident to register and carry a certificate of

Lilly Ong Hing Fong, circa late 1960s to 1980s. —North Las Vegas Library
Photograph Collection [00277 009670], UNLV Libraries Special Collections & Archives

residence or face arrest and possible deportation. These later evolved into Alien Registration Receipt Cards or "green cards." Even Chinese Americans who were citizens risked expulsion or lengthy detention if they left the country and tried to return. The Geary Act regulated Chinese immigration into the 1920s.

No wonder the Chinese population in the United States declined. In 1880, the Chinese population in Nevada was over five thousand. Ten years later, less than three thousand remained. Carson City alone had been home to nearly one thousand Chinese residents. Chinese workers had originally been recruited to the territory in 1857 to dig a ditch from the Carson River to the mouth of Gold Cañon Mine. Some stayed in the area and opened restaurants and laundries. With the onset of the transcontinental railroad construction in 1863, many worked for the Central Pacific Railroad that headed east. But the rise of labor unions and the racial unease after the Civil War precipitated anti-immigrant feelings by the 1870s, and the Chinese were the first ethnic group to be targeted.

By 1900, only 1,276 Chinese still lived in Nevada and most of these were men. Chinese cultural values as well as financial difficulties prevented most women from traveling alone to "the Gold Mountain," the name originally given to California and later used in reference to the western regions of North America (although Nevada was sometimes referred to as "the Silver Mountain"). If in the country, Chinese women could not attain citizenship through marriage to an American citizen.

More discriminatory laws were adopted in the early twentieth century. The federal government created laws that excluded not only the Chinese, but all people of Asian descent. Some states banned Asians from owning land. The Expatriation Act of March 2, 1907, mandated that "any American woman who marries a foreigner shall take the nationality of her husband." So by saying "I do," a woman lost her American citizenship. She could become a citizen again if her husband became a naturalized citizen of the United States or if she went through the naturalization process. Laws fluctuated into the 1930s. For example, by 1932, a Chinese woman born in Hawaii could obtain citizenship only if she was born before 1900.

Luckily, Lilly Ong Hing did not have to experience the attitudes of this era. In 1930, Lilly's mother, Helen Annie Soo Hoo, took her five-year-old daughter and three of her other children (Minnie, Ollie, and baby Holie) from their home in Superior, Arizona, to Canton, China, where they lived for seven years. Lilly's grandmother was ill and needed a caretaker, and the United States was a difficult place to live during the Great Depression. In Chinese school Lilly studied the teachings and memorized the last will and testament of Sun Yat-Sen, who is known as the Father of Modern China. He was the first president and a founder of the Republic of China. She liked his idea that the "whole world is one family." She also learned about the ancient Chinese dynasties. Lilly used an abacus (a frame with rows of beads) to count and she created beautiful letters with calligraphy. She played games with marbles and checkers and enjoyed hopscotch outside. She also became an ace Ping-Pong player. Unlike other Chinese Americans, Lilly was well grounded in her parents' culture.

In 1937, when China and Japan began the second Sino-Japanese War, Lilly's father, Ong Chung Hing, brought the family back to the United States via the Dollar Line passenger ship SS *President Hoover*. Luckily, they traveled before that ship wrecked in December of that year. In explaining the move, Ong cited Confucius, someone Lilly had also learned about in China: "Confucius said education is the equalizer of all. It knows no distinction in class. If I give you money, you would spend it. So I am going to give you an education that is going to last for life."

Although generally only sons acquired education in the Chinese tradition, all ten of Ong's children received support and earned college degrees in different fields. After graduating from Superior High School (1945), Lilly earned a degree from Arizona State University in Tempe in 1949. She was a member and served as president of the Kappa Theta

Sorority and is pictured in that group in the 1948 *Sahuaro* yearbook. She participated in service projects, such as sending holiday boxes to the local state hospital. According to the 1949 university yearbook, the group sponsored a project to send boxes to needy families in China. Lilly's appreciation of education and dedication to charitable giving began at a young age and would continue.

———•••———

Lilly Ong Hing's father had immigrated to the United States from China in 1912. He settled in Phoenix, Arizona, where he opened restaurants with other members of the family. In 1921, he started the American Kitchen Restaurant, which served food and sold groceries in the small mining town of Superior, Arizona. Although Lilly's mother was born in the United States in 1901, she returned to China in 1903 with her family to care for an ailing relative. In 1921, around age twenty, she became a picture bride, a woman wed to a man without ever meeting him in person prior to the marriage. The traditional Buddhist ceremony was held in China, where Helen remained for two more years in her husband's village while Ong built them a home in Arizona.

Helen finally arrived in San Francisco on July 1, 1924, after a twenty-one-day sea voyage on the Japanese passenger liner SS *Tenyo Maru*. Lilly, born June 17, 1925, was the oldest of their ten children. After graduating from Arizona State University, Lilly taught elementary students in Pasadena, California, and pursued a master's degree at the University of Southern California. There, she met Wing Gay Fong at a church picnic in Chinatown. He was attending Woodbury College in Burbank, California.

Born on August 27, 1925, the son of a Cantonese rice farmer, Wing was sent by his mother to live with his uncles in Las Vegas after his father died in 1939. He was thirteen, but knowing no English, he was put in a lower grade at school. Wing taught himself to speak English through the use of English-Chinese dictionaries, so he was allowed to skip grades. He worked after school and on weekends as a dishwasher at his uncles' restaurant, the Silver Café, which they had opened at the corner of North First and Fremont Streets in 1933. They had gained experience when working as cooks for the Union Pacific Railroad. One of the largest restaurants in town at the time, it had an all-electric kitchen, twenty-four-hour Chinese-American food service, and slot machines for customer entertainment. In the 1930s and 1940s, it would also deliver food to patrons of gambling establishments nearby.

Wing graduated with honors from Las Vegas High School in 1946. He considered becoming a doctor and started taking premed college classes at the University of Nevada in Reno, but switched his major to business administration when he discovered he was allergic to formaldehyde. In 1950, he earned a BA in Business Administration from Woodbury College in Los Angeles. Right after he graduated, he and Lilly married in the garden of the sixteen-story Hotel Westward Ho in Phoenix, Arizona, on July 16, 1950. Many members of her family were in the wedding party that celebrated in the elegant Art Deco-styled hotel, which advertised that all of its 350 rooms were air-conditioned, a rarity at the time. Lilly finished her MA degree many years later.

Lilly had reservations about moving to Wing's hometown, because Las Vegas in 1950 was still viewed as a "frontier" gambling mecca. But she reluctantly conceded and went with her husband. Although he felt he was discriminated against for some jobs, Wing's business degree finally got him a position as the accountant and manager of the Pioneer Distributing Company and Las Vegas Bottling Company. He also opened a grocery store that had slot machines for its patrons. Wing often gave free food to those who gambled away their food allowance. His son, Kenneth Wayne Fong, born in 1955, recalled one family story about his father's generosity: "He had the compassion to give back the money so she could have groceries for her family. He didn't like seeing people lose their money."

The couple soon collaborated with Wing's uncles, who closed the Silver Café after twenty-one years in business to open Fongs' Garden restaurant on Labor Day in 1955 on East Charleston Boulevard. The quirky pagoda entrance, made of oxidized copper and imported furnishings from Hong Kong, enticed people to check it out, and the reasonably priced, tasty Cantonese cuisine quickly made the restaurant a favorite place for local residents. In 1959 Harry Reid, US Senator from Nevada from 1987 to 2017, took his new wife there for their wedding dinner because it was so popular. The restaurant was one of the first businesses to advertise on television. Its menu told the diner:

> "It is a JOYOUS OCCASION for us to serve you. In order to serve our Chinese cuisine in the finest way possible, we cook all our dishes to order. However, we suggest that until you become familiar with our menu, you are welcome to consult our host or management who will recommend not only palatable dishes that complement each other, but also quantities that will ensure a satisfying dinner for you and your friends. This is only a suggestion, and we thought you would like to know about it."

The restaurant became the cornerstone for a small Chinatown in that area of Las Vegas in the 1950s. Today Chinatown Plaza, with its traditional welcome arch, is located on Spring Mountain Road not far from the Strip. In October 1999, Kenny Guinn, who was beginning his term as Governor of Nevada that year, officially designated the area as Chinatown.

Wing also became active in banking and acquiring more real estate. In 1956, he and Lilly felt they could start giving back to the community. Lilly and Wing donated one day's business profits to the library at the newly founded Southern Division of the University of Nevada, which evolved into the Nevada Southern University and is now known as the University of Nevada, Las Vegas (UNLV). Their daughter, Susan Kay Fong, was born on August 5, 1957. In the 1960s, Wing started Wing Fong Enterprises, which developed and built office and other commercial buildings as well as shopping centers. His son recalls, "And being a pioneer here, he knew a lot of the early business people, so he had a lot of good contacts." These served him well over the years.

Lilly interviewed for a position as a schoolteacher, but wasn't hired by the superintendent of the Clark County School District despite the fact that she had teaching experience and graduate education. She appealed the decision to the School Board of Trustees, and they directed the superintendent to hire her. Lilly became the first Asian American teacher in the Clark County school system in 1950 and was recognized as an outstanding teacher in 1952. She taught for five years at Fifth Street School and West Charleston Elementary and then opted to stay home with her two young children. Both she and Wing became naturalized US citizens, and they embraced their dual cultures. They built an Asian-style family home on Silver Avenue, near present-day Interstate 15, with their last name in the red and gold Chinese character on the garage door and a dragon on the mailbox. But in outings to Mount Charleston or Lake Mead with Kenneth and Susan, Wing would barbeque steaks—an American pastime—and for dessert they would toast marshmallows.

In 1963, Lilly started teaching the first Chinese language classes in Las Vegas. Governor Paul Laxalt (1967–1971) appointed Lilly to the Commission on the Status of Women, where she served as Education Vice Chairman. She served as state president of the American Association of University Women from 1972 to 1973. The following year, because her family and friends went door-to-door campaigning on her behalf, she was elected to the Board of Regents for the University and Community College System of Nevada, upsetting incumbent William Morris who held the post from 1970 to 1974. Lilly was the first Chinese woman—and the first Asian woman—to hold such an elected position in the nation.

Lilly supported the increased development of UNLV in order for it to keep pace with the swelling population growth of Las Vegas. She and Wing established an endowment fund for a Chinese language program at UNLV in the College of Liberal Arts. The Wing and Lilly Fong Scholarship Endowment at UNLV assists students studying the Chinese language with $500 awards. Lilly donated her per diem regent stipend for travel expenses to that cause. She was instrumental in saving Tonopah Hall, built in 1966 as a dormitory, from destruction. She convinced the board that recruiting out-of-state students would fill the residence facility. As James "Bucky" Buchanan, an attorney who served on the Board of Regents with Lilly for ten years stated: "She took a hands-on approach and was totally dedicated to improving the image of UNLV. She really understood finances and had a great perspective for picking presidents and other people for key jobs."

Lilly also supported programs and scholarships that encouraged senior citizens and older students to complete their education, whether at the university or community college level. She personally exemplified this effort in 1980 when, at age fifty-five, she finished her Master's Degree in Education. In 1982, she was chosen UNLV Alumnus of the Year. Lilly became a lecturer in the UNLV Continuing Education Program, specializing in Asian languages and religion. In November 1984, after losing a close race for reelection to the regent position she had held for ten years, Lilly vowed that her dedication to higher education would continue. She stated: "I am proud of my record and accomplishments and I will continue to serve our university and community college in any way I can." This promise manifested in the creation of the Excellence in Student Teaching Awards and the Lilly Fong Distinguished Professor Award in the College of Education at UNLV.

Lilly also supported the arts. She was a member of the Las Vegas Symphony Board of Directors. She was instrumental in persuading Judy Bayley and Artemus Ham, Jr. to become major donors for the construction of a performing arts center at UNLV. It opened in 1970 and included the Judy Bayley Theatre and the Artemus Ham

Concert Hall. The Rita Abbey original murals in the performing arts center and the thirty-eight-foot-tall Claes Oldenburg flashlight sculpture, erected in 1981 and which sits in a plaza near this complex, exist because of Lilly's fundraising efforts. She also helped acquire $750,000 to build the Alta Ham Fine Arts Building, which houses the art, dance, music, and theater arts departments.

From 1982 to 1984, Lilly also spearheaded fundraising projects for other disciplines. She helped raise $3 million for Beam Hall, where the Business and Hotel Administration programs are located, as well as for the Engineering and Computer Science Schools. In 1985, she and Wing donated $150,000 to the UNLV Foundation, which was used for many campus improvements.

As a graduate of Arizona State University (ASU), Lilly did not forget her own alma mater; she created the Warner-Fong Fellowship at that institution in 1986. It honored Ila Marie White Warner, whose service to the Las Vegas community and dedication to ASU inspired Lilly. Ila was a fellow teacher and a member of the Francisco Garcés chapter of the National Society Daughters of the American Revolution (DAR). She was instrumental in the creation of the monument that commemorates Padre Francisco Garcés as the "first recorded white man to enter Nevada," which can be found in the Lorenzi Park Rose Garden in Las Vegas. Ila also served as state regent for the Nevada State Society DAR from 1964 to 1966 and established the Ila Warner Scholarship Fund which, to date—many years after her death in 1988—annually provides a $500 award for a full-time student attending an institution of higher education in Nevada. The fellowship also honored Lilly's parents, Ong Chung and Helen Hing, for their "love, sacrifice and the educational encouragement," which fostered a love of learning in all ten of their children and that Lilly shared with her own children, who are both college graduates. The Warner-Fong Fellowship is awarded each year to an incoming freshman or transfer student who is pursuing a Bachelor of Arts in Asian Studies.

Both Lilly and Wing have received numerous awards as well as recognition for their many years of community service and generous donations. In 1985, the UNLV geoscience building was named after Lilly because $50,000 of her donation went to upgrade that facility. In 1991, the Clark County School District opened the Wing and Lilly Fong Elementary School, located at 2200 James Bilbray Drive in Las Vegas, the first public school named after Chinese Americans. The Board of Regents of the Nevada System of Higher Education designated Lilly and her husband as Distinguished Nevadans for Southern Nevada in 1998.

Lilly died on March 20, 2002, at age seventy-six. Wing honored her memory and their Chinese heritage when he donated in both of their names to the Asian Art Museum in San Francisco, California, in 2003. Wing died three years after Lilly, on May 22, 2005. In Wing's obituary, family members suggested that donations in his memory be made to the Lilly Fong Language Fund at UNLV. The couple is buried together in the Garden of Roses section at Bunkers Eden Vale Memorial Park in Las Vegas, a tribute to their fifty-two-year marriage.

Lilly is remembered as a philanthropist who gave both time and money. A friend who knew her from the First Presbyterian Church in Las Vegas observed: "She was always willing to give of herself and her finances to help anyone, especially if it dealt with education or children." Perhaps the importance her father placed on education while she was growing up precipitated this lifelong dedication. She was also keenly aware of her heritage. Pat Goodall, who served as the President of UNLV from 1979 to 1984, remembered: "Both of them (Lilly and Wing) were always very interested in the role of minorities, especially the Chinese in Nevada. Anytime someone talked about the history or wrote about the history of Nevada they would make sure the history of Chinese workers was well represented."

President and editor of the *Las Vegas Sun*, Brian Greenspun, whose family was close to the Fong family, probably summed up the lasting community sentiment the best: "Our respect for Wing and Lilly was total." When the *Las Vegas Review-Journal* completed its *First 100* three-part newspaper project in 1999 (which also was published as a book)—of the first one hundred important people who shaped southern Nevada—it is assuredly fitting that Lilly and Wing were selected out of the over three hundred nominations in recognition of their personal philanthropy and altruistic concern for others. Lilly spent her life putting into practice the "whole world is one family" philosophy she learned as a child.

11

VELMA BRONN JOHNSTON
(1912–1977)

Wild Horse Annie's Fight to Save the Mustang

A lovely spring day in 1950 started off as a normal workday for Velma Bronn Johnston. The twenty-six mile drive west from her home on the Double Lazy Heart Ranch to her job as an executive secretary at an insurance company in Reno, Nevada, usually took her about an hour; the twisting gravel roads forced her to be cautious. On this morning, she found herself following an old truck with a canvas top and wooden slats on the sides. It wasn't unusual to see trailers moving horses in this rural ranching community, and Velma stayed a safe distance behind until passing seemed possible. Then she did a double take. Blood was dripping out of the back of the vehicle when the driver hit the brakes.

You could say Velma Bronn Johnston owed her life to mustangs. As a baby, her father, Joseph Bronn, had been given the milk of a mustang mare while the family traveled across the Nevada deserts in a covered wagon in 1885. Velma was not going to ignore what she saw. She followed the horse trailer to a stockyard where horses were held before being killed to make pet food in Sparks, four miles east of downtown Reno. When the tailgate of the trailer dropped, Velma knew instantly what had happened. A young colt had been sandwiched between two adult stallions. In the tight space, as the

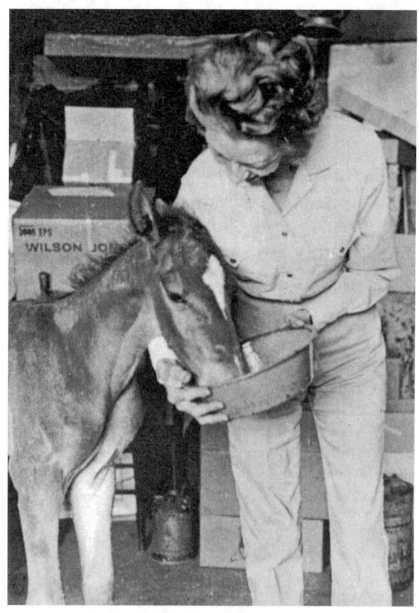

Velma Bronn Johnston feeding a foal. —Courtesy of the Nevada Historical Society, Bio-J-101

horses jockeyed for room, the colt had been trampled to death by the bigger horses.

Velma wanted answers. Why had this happened? Where did these horses come from and why were they being slaughtered? Five days later, she attended a meeting at the Reno office of the Bureau of Land Management, the agency that managed wild horses. That day changed her life forever.

———•••———

Velma Ione Bronn was born in Reno on March 5, 1912, to Joseph A. and Gertrude "Trudy" Hattie Clay Bronn. Her father had been born in Ione, Nevada, in Nye County, which is how she got her middle name. She was the oldest of the four children: three girls (Velma, Loreene Marie, born in 1922, and Betty Jo, born in 1929), and a boy (Jack, born in 1915). Velma's father was a drover—a person who moves animals such as sheep, cattle, and horses "on the hoof" from place to place—and he also broke mustangs, America's wild horses. Velma loved to be outside and watch her father train horses on their Lazy Heart Ranch, but she also liked to draw and play dress-up games at their house on Washington Street in Reno. Schoolwork, such as penmanship exercises and matching words and meanings, were easy for her. She loved to listen to her teacher read aloud, especially poetry. But Velma was a shy child and being called upon in class to verbally answer a question left her tongue-tied and embarrassed.

Disease took the lives of many children in this era. When Velma was eleven, she contracted polio, a disease that can paralyze its victims. Because her family had used up their resources on hip problems that Jack encountered, Velma was sent to the Children's Hospital in San Francisco, a facility that treated the poor. She was fitted with a three-quarter-body cast that went from the top of her head to below her hips to prevent her body from twisting to one side. Her parents couldn't afford to stay with her, so Velma had a lonely six-month hospitalization.

When the cast was finally removed, Velma's parents were stunned. The cast had stilted her growth. She had multiple physical ailments, including a drooping left shoulder, displaced jaw, misaligned teeth, and scoliosis (curvature of the spine). It took months for her to recover after she returned home in the spring of 1924. Her mother removed all of the mirrors in the house and told her daughter, "When you get down to the wire, you tighten your belt, hold your head high and squarely face whatever is in store."

Velma had to be strong to endure the isolation caused by her disfigurement. Other children now either shunned Velma or called her cruel names, but a boy named Walter Baring remained her friend. Her beloved father became withdrawn around her, too, and in 1927, when Jack died of meningitis, her father became even more reclusive and favored the younger girls. Velma coped by daydreaming about her future. She wanted to become a secretary to an important man and have a husband "who loved horses only slightly less than he loved me." She longed for a ranch, a barn, and many children. For a disfigured young woman, these were very big goals.

Velma learned how to sew, and made clothes that would help bring positive attention to her thin body. She also learned how to hide her poor posture: "By concentrating on it very hard, I learned to hold my shoulders level, and if I was careful and did not stand squarely before a person but rather slightly sideways, the difference in me was not so noticeable. Or so I have told myself. Good grooming and stylish wardrobes had a tendency to draw attention from that about which I was so shy."

With top marks in typing, dictation, and shorthand, Velma graduated from high school in 1930. She immediately got a job as a stenographer at the Farmers and Merchants Bank (later First National Bank of Nevada) in Reno. Her boss, Gordon Harris, was expected to go far in the business community, so Velma figured she had achieved her goal of working for an important man. She called him "my executive." Although only 23 percent of Nevada homes had telephones then, it was quickly becoming an essential business tool. Velma felt comfortable with telephone transactions because customers could not see her physical disability. Immersing herself in her work, she joined the Reno chapter of Executive Secretaries Incorporated. This membership helped her make friends with others in her field and was also a source for information about the local business community.

In 1936, Velma went with her mother to Saint Mary's Hospital to visit her father, who had injured himself while repairing a truck. She was startled to hear loud laughter coming from his room. Her father was being entertained by his roommate, a construction worker named Charles Clyde Johnston. A heavy ceramic jug had fallen three floors and landed on Charles's head at a Reno building site, so he was recovering from a fractured skull. Born December 14, 1899, in Macon, West Virginia, Charlie (as he preferred to be called) was a World War I veteran who had come to Reno for a fast divorce. He stayed there, sometimes working as a horseman and tracker. Although he was ten years older, he and Velma hit it off, and they eloped on a hot Sunday in July 1937. Velma had to keep the marriage a secret (even from her family) so she could keep her job. The common belief at this time was that once a woman married, she should stay at home and her husband would support her. Charlie continued to live in a rooming house, and Velma lived at home.

Charlie found a job the following year as a deputy sheriff in Gabbs in Nye County. Now they could finally disclose their marriage, and Velma would still be able to work outside the home as a secretary for a local mining company due to the lack of residents in the rural community. Velma's mother insisted they have a formal wedding, so they remarried at Velma's parents' home on August 14, 1938.

Life in Gabbs was not luxurious. They lived in a two-room shack that lacked what we consider basic necessities today—electricity, running water, indoor plumbing, and adequate heat. Gabbs became important to the war effort in 1941, due to the mining of magnesium, but when the war need for that metal was over, Gabbs collapsed as a town. Charlie and Velma moved back to Reno. She now was able to work as a stenographer, and Charlie fixed motorcycles. They purchased sixteen acres of land outside of Sparks and named their new home the Double Lazy Heart Ranch. Her old boss, Gordon Harris, opened his own insurance company and hired Velma to work for him. At this time, Charlie would drive Velma into Reno for her job on Monday mornings and take her father back with him to their ranch to build their home. Velma would stay for the week with her mother. While construction was occurring, she only went home on weekends.

Soon afterwards, in 1950, she saw the truck with the hurt and dying mustang on its way to the slaughterhouse. Velma started attending the meetings of the Bureau of Land Management (BLM), the government agency that managed much of the public land in Nevada. She was appalled to hear a BLM officer state that from 1946 to 1950, over one hundred thousand horses had been removed from Nevada and made into pet food. He also estimated that by 1950 fewer than four thousand mustangs would remain in the whole state.

Velma was livid. She decided to start an advocacy group to protect the mustangs. Charlie helped her, and the horses became their family, although they also opened their home on weekends and summers to provide city children a ranch experience. In 1952, due to their efforts, Storey County passed a law that outlawed roundups of horses by aircraft. It wasn't until 1955 that the State of Nevada banned the use of aircraft to capture wild horses on state and private land. Federal lands constituted 86 percent of the land in the state, however, so Velma needed to get similar legislation at the national level. As she stated: "Since the wild horses and burros are part of our national heritage, belonging to all the people of America, and inhabit the public domain that also belongs to all the people of America, I believe the only way to guarantee the survival of these animals that are a symbol of the freedom upon which our country was founded, is to continue to work for federal legislation toward that end."

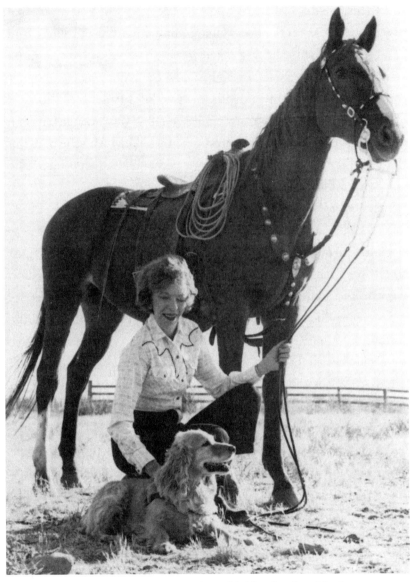

Velma Bronn Johnston with her dog and holding the reins of her horse.
—Courtesy of the Nevada Historical Society, Bio-J-00102

Many people opposed her work of protecting the wild horses and, spitefully, started calling her "Wild Horse Annie" and sending her threats. Velma didn't care, but she began to hold a gun when answering knocks on the door. Charlie had taught her to shoot, and she was a crack shot, having taken the head off a rattlesnake more than once. The BLM was her biggest adversary, but according to her mother, she learned to work with them without violence: "I think it was her ability to listen, because I think you find out a whole lot more in this old world by listening than you do by talking. And she had that ability to listen, and to not be unfair. If someone had a problem, she was always willing to listen to see if it could be changed."

The *Denver Post* newspaper helped Velma's cause when it sent Robert O'Brien to interview her and write an article that was published in *Reader's Digest* in January 1958. "The Mustangs' Last Stand" sold ten million copies a month, and thirty-eight million people in the United States and around the world read about Velma. O'Brien introduced her as, "The most tireless, outspoken friend the mustang ever had is Mrs. Velma B. Johnston. . . . She stands five foot six in her high-heeled riding boots and weighs a spunky 108 pounds. But her diminutive size has not kept her from waging a bitter battle for the country's mustangs—so bitter in fact, that friends and opponents now refer to her as 'Wild Horse Annie.'"

Letters flooded in. As Velma recalled, "Offers to help have come from every state, and people in all walks of life have joined the fight— ministers, housewives, students, teachers, sportsmen, the nuns in a convent in the East, a blind man who had read the story in Braille, men in the US Armed Forces in far-away places, lawyers, doctors— and people from all ages . . . At least my efforts have accomplished this much: mustang fever is raging!"

Velma received letters from outside the United States as well. The Reno post office delivered many with vague address information such as:

Mrs. Velma Johnston
Ranch Woman from State of Nevada
Lobbying for Law in US Congress to protect wild horses
Somewhere in Nevada, U.S.A.

Velma responded to each letter, sending packets of background information at her own expense. An article by the Associated Press on July 15, 1959, noted, "Seldom has an issue touched such a responsive chord."

With help from her childhood friend Walter Baring, who had become a representative for Nevada in the US Congress, the first federal law to protect wild horses was finally passed. Known as the Wild Horse Annie Act (Public Law 86-234), it was signed into law by President Dwight D. Eisenhower on September 8, 1959. It banned the use of any type of motorized vehicle, aircraft, or land vehicle, as well as the poisoning of water holes to capture or kill free-running horses and burros. For her efforts to achieve this legislation, in 1959 Velma became the first woman to receive the prestigious Angell Memorial Gold Medal from the Massachusetts branch of the Society for the Prevention of Cruelty to Animals.

Three years later, in December 1962, the Department of the Interior created the first wild horse refuge in the country. Located in the high-desert terrain of Nellis Air Force Base outside of Las Vegas, Nevada, salt lick stations were set up near springs and waterholes. Because the military establishment is off limits to the public, the horses were not harassed. It took three years for another one to be created in Utah. The Cedar Mountains Herd Management Area is located fifty miles west of Salt Lake City and includes almost 180,000 acres.

During the same time, Velma continued her job as a secretary and had to nurse Charlie, who had become terminally ill with emphysema, probably from smoking hand-rolled cigarettes for years. He died on March 14, 1964, and was buried in Mountain View Cemetery in Reno. To cope with losing her partner of twenty-seven years, Velma focused on her daily work and distanced herself somewhat from the horse protection movement.

Then fate stepped in to introduce Velma to children's author Marguerite Henry. The two became friends, and Marguerite decided to write a book about Velma's efforts to save wild horses. *Mustang: Wild Spirit of the West* brought the issue to children. Sometimes Velma would appear with Marguerite at book promotion events, but she would also make presentations by herself. The book sold around six hundred thousand copies when it was released in 1966. It garnered the National Cowboy and Western Heritage Museum's 1967 Western Heritage Award for Outstanding Juvenile Book and the Oklahoma Library Association's 1970 Sequoyah Book Award. The book continues to sell many copies annually and is lauded as "a story of the preservation of wild animals and truly moving as a story of a dauntless woman."

The children who read the book became part of Velma's "Pencil War" and sent letters to politicians on behalf of saving the wild horses and burros. Teachers used the issue as a civics lesson, sometimes using the curriculum Velma created for the book. Members of the US Congress recalled that they received more correspondence on this issue than any other, save the Vietnam War. No longer the shy girl who hated to speak in public, Velma testified before the members of Congress. Finally, on December 15, 1971, President Richard Nixon signed into law Walter Baring's Wild and Free-Roaming Horses and Burros Act (Public Law 92-195). Unanimously passed by Congress, it banned the capture, branding, and death of wild horses on public lands and recognized them as "living symbols of the historic and pioneer spirit of the West." President Nixon credited the grassroots public support led by Velma for the political drive to get the measure approved.

Velma opted to retire from the only full-time paid job she ever had on May 15, 1974. Now she could devote herself fully to the preservation of the wild horses. Even after so many years, her zeal continued. "You occasionally see one, and it's the thrill of a lifetime," she remarked. "But mostly all you ever see is a cloud of dust after they are gone. It's their stubborn ability to survive that makes them so remarkable."

Velma fought high blood pressure and a heart condition, but that is not what finally took her life. On June 27, 1977, at age sixty-five, Velma died of lung cancer. She is buried alongside her parents, husband, and brother in the Mountain View Cemetery in Reno. Three horses prance on her tombstone, appearing to honor their champion.

Velma's passing was noted in the nation's largest newspapers. Every obituary praised her efforts to protect wild horses. The *Reno Evening Gazette* stated: "Annie's detractors would have undoubtedly preferred her to be weak and sentimental. What they got from Annie was a tough, hard-headed realist who marshaled her facts, set about her campaign to protect wild horses with steely determination, and who often had a gun handy for self defense."

Even after her death, Velma's influence can be seen in various ways. By following her efforts, many young men and women were introduced to the subjects of biology, land management, public administration, and public policy, and this led some to pursue careers in these fields. Little Book Cliffs Wild Horse Area was established in the mountains north of Grand Junction, Colorado. When it opened on November 7, 1980, the area was dedicated to Mrs. Velma B. "Wild Horse Annie" Johnston, as is inscribed on a monument near the entrance at Indian Park.

The two advocacy organizations that Velma helped establish and then worked with—the International Society for the Protection of Mustangs and Burros and the Wild Horse Organizational Assistance (cleverly shortened to WHOA)—are both still in existence. They continue the work that Velma began.

Modern viewers can see some of the horse roundup methods used by "mustangers"—which Velma fought against—in the 1961

Western *The Misfits*, which is still available for screening. Velma was partly the inspiration for Marilyn Monroe's character in the film. Velma also portrayed herself in the 1973 Western *Running Wild*. A television movie called *Wild Horse Annie*, with Betty White playing Velma, was filmed by CBS in 1978 but was never aired. In 2012, the Hallmark Movie Channel filmed *Wild Horse Annie* with Wendie Malick in the starring role.

Sierra Magazine writer Harold Walter summed up Velma's dedication to saving wild horses from extinction as follows: "History is made in many odd ways. It is unusual that a peaceful Nevada woman should have stirred the world to the diminishing beat of the wild mustang herds. She made the defiant scream of the stallions a trumpet of protest." In June 1989, US Senator from Nevada, Harry Reid, introduced legislation to designate March 21, the first day of spring, as National Free-Roaming Wild Horse and Burro Day. While never officially designated, that day can still be used to honor the many ups and downs that Velma endured in her quest to save the mustangs—those magnificent animals that embody the spirit of freedom that was found in the Old West.

12

SARANN KNIGHT PREDDY
(1920–2014)

Luck Found the Lady
Who Never Said "No"

President Harry S. Truman signed Executive Order 9981, which prohibited racial discrimination in the armed forces, on July 26, 1948. However, segregation was still widely accepted throughout America in the 1950s. Las Vegas was no exception. A March 1954 article by James R. Goodrich in *Ebony* magazine included the observations of a black entertainer who visited the city: "It's like some place in Mississippi—downright prejudice." He added that a black person "finds little welcome anywhere . . . . barred from practically every place whites go for entertainment or services. He cannot live outside a segregated, slum-like community. He is relegated to the most menial jobs . . . . Vegas is as bad as towns come . . . . Rate[s] no better than second-class citizenship there."

Due to its discriminatory practices, Nevada became known throughout the United States as the "Mississippi of the West." African Americans were not allowed on the Strip in Las Vegas unless they were hired to provide entertainment or work menial jobs in the hotels and casinos. Big name black performers, such as Nat King Cole, Lena Horne, Pearl Bailey, and Duke Ellington, could entertain white audiences in the casino showrooms but were not permitted to stay in the hotels. Sammy Davis Jr. once noted, "In Vegas for 20

Sarann Knight Preddy, circa 1979. —North Las Vegas Library Photograph Collection [00277 000457], UNLV Libraries Special Collections & Archives

minutes, our skin had no color. Then the second we stepped off the stage, we were colored again . . . the other acts could gamble or sit in the lounge and have a drink, but we had to leave through the kitchen with the garbage."

They stayed in Westside, the largely African American section of the city. Although Westside lacked facilities found elsewhere, such as running water, working sewage lines, and paved streets, it was a close-knit community of about ten square blocks that supported churches and schools for its residents. Jackson Street, also known as the Black Strip, hosted black-owned businesses and clubs, such as the Cotton Club and Brown Derby.

On May 24, 1955, when the Moulin Rouge Hotel and Casino opened, the color green became more important than skin tone. Conveniently situated on Bonanza Road, between the mainly white boundary of the Strip and the black establishments of Westside, the Moulin Rouge was the first racially integrated hotel casino in the United States. Although the ownership was white—except for the alleged 2 percent share owned by former heavyweight boxing champion Joe Lewis—the opening and success of the Moulin Rouge gained national recognition and brought the hope of integration to the Las Vegas community. *Life* magazine ran a photo of dancers from the club on its cover on June 20, 1955. Prominent white entertainers, such as Judy Garland, Jack Benny, George Burns, and Frank Sinatra, would drop in and sometimes perform, boosting its popularity. In a nod to its cabaret namesake in Paris, France, all of the security guards wore exact replicas of the French *gendarme* (police) uniforms.

This spark of change didn't last long. After less than six months of operation, employees coming to work found padlocks on the doors. No one knows exactly what caused its demise. However, the short but energetic days of the Moulin Rouge truly helped promote the civil rights movement in Las Vegas. Its activities and features had included an integrated swimming pool, and many of those who enjoyed the amenities, as well as those who were employed by the 110-room hotel, became activists and strong supporters of integration. These included James McMillan and Charles West, inhabitants of Westside, who became Nevada's first black dentist and physician, respectively. In March 1960, they threatened a mass protest march down the Strip to disrupt business if civic leaders didn't meet with them to negotiate the end of segregation on the Strip. The meeting was held on March 26 in the coffee shop in the closed Moulin Rouge. Governor Grant Sawyer, Las Vegas mayor Oran Gragson, and other key businessmen in the city met with representatives from the National Association for

Moulin Rouge Hotel and Casino on May 23, 1955. —Don T. Walker Collection [000042], UNLV Libraries Special Collections & Archives

the Advancement of Colored People (NAACP) and worked out an agreement that desegregated the city. It is aptly known as the Moulin Rouge Agreement.

Sarann Knight Preddy, the first African American woman to hold a Nevada gaming license, wanted to help the Moulin Rouge rise again as a working casino. She seemed like the perfect choice to make this happen. Her father had helped construct the casino by supplying cinder blocks from a factory that he owned in the 1950s, and Sarann had attended its opening in 1955. From 1985 to 1997, along with her husband, Joe, and son, James, she put in an enormous amount of time and effort to revitalize this history-making locale. They offered live entertainment and Cajun and American food, hoping to draw the sizeable crowds of the past. By 1993, gamblers could enjoy fifteen slot machines and three gaming tables.

But by this time, the licensing process in the state had become much more complicated and they only received limited licenses for six-month periods. The NAACP interceded and managed to get them annual renewals. They also received a grant from the State of Nevada, along with some federal financing, to assist the Nevada Historical Society in constructing an onsite museum to commemorate the original Moulin Rouge. But the federal money required $2 million in matching funds and banks weren't willing to underwrite the project. Even though Sarann sold her own home to raise money for the venture, the dream of reopening the casino finally died. However, Sarann did get the Moulin Rouge recognized on the National Register of Historic Places in 1992.

Fires in 2003 and 2009 left the buildings of the hotel and casino severely damaged. Luckily, the neon sign designed by Betty Willis, who also created the iconic Welcome to Las Vegas sign at the south end of the Strip, was saved and can be seen at the local Neon Museum, along with advertising signs from many long-gone Las Vegas buildings. To maintain the gaming license for the site, gambling occurs every two years via video poker machines that are trucked in for eight hours. In

October 2017, Clark County offered to buy the site for $6.2 million in order to construct new administrative offices. But after getting public input, this offer was withdrawn. Locals continue to hope that the site's place in history can be maintained.

While nothing but memories and photographs now remain to showcase the original hotel casino—which cost $3.5 million to build and rivaled other properties on the Strip with its nearly 89,000-square-foot club—the importance of the site to the history of civil rights in the United States lives on. For Sarann, it was only one of the many influential activities she participated in to promote racial equality in her lifetime.

———•••———

Eva Louise Chiles (spelled "Childs" in some records)—or Sarann as she came to be known—was born on July 27, 1920, in Eufaula, Oklahoma, a small, diverse town in the eastern part of the state. Her parents, Carl James Chiles (1899–1984) and Hattie Crabtree Chiles (1902–1998) were biracial. Her mother was African American and Creek Indian. Her father was African American and Spanish. Her brother, Clarence, was born in 1922. The 1930 US Census records her name as Eva Louise, and although there is no official record of a name change, she opted to change her name. In the 1940 US Census, she is listed as Sarah Ann, and she sometimes used the name Sarah Louise. She most often spelled her name "Sarann," but always insisted that it not be shortened to either Sara or Ann.

Her family was financially sound due to her father's job as a stoneworker on construction projects, along with other ventures. While she was growing up, he owned several businesses, including a restaurant, a general store, and a meat market. At age thirteen, Sarann, inspired by his entrepreneurial spirit, started selling pig's feet for five cents each and had difficulty keeping up with the customer demand for this Southern delicacy.

Her father also played guitar professionally; she probably developed her love of music through him. She learned to play every type of saxophone available. Sarann's mother, a homemaker, raised many children from the extended family as well as her own. A loving but strict disciplinarian, she taught the children under her care honesty and morality.

Sarann attended school in Eufaula through sixth grade. Despite competing with the other twenty-nine students in her school, Sarann recalls that the teacher gave a lot of individual attention: "One day she took me horseback riding. Neither she nor I knew much about horses, but we both wanted to try it. Well, we were going down a hill and the horse started galloping so fast that she could not stop it. The horse threw us both and I was unconscious for one or two days. I have not been on a horse since." Her parents valued education, so when she was twelve, Sarann was sent to attend Dunbar High School in Okmulgee, Oklahoma. This school had over a thousand students and Sarann loved performing for them. She often played her saxophone and acted in school plays. Her biggest problem was dating. She had so many relatives in the area that she had to be careful she didn't go out with a cousin.

In 1937, soon after she graduated, Sarann married twenty-five-year-old Luther Walker. Her parents did not approve of the marriage, due to their eight-year age difference, so they eloped. Their first two children, James Edward (1939) and Richard Luther (1941), were born in Oklahoma. In the 1940 US Census, Luther is listed as working as a hotel porter. Sarann, Luther, and her father moved to Las Vegas in 1942. Her mother brought James and Richard with her when she moved later.

Two more children, Janice Marie (1943) and Glynn Davis (1944), were born in Las Vegas. According to Sarann, the town was "absolutely nothing." This may explain why her mother did not unpack her suitcases for their entire first year there. For a while, Luther and Sarann's father worked at the Midway City Basic

Magnesium Inc. plant, where magnesium was processed to make a vital aluminum alloy used in airplane construction during World War II (1941–1945). Mainly composed of government housing, Midway City's name was changed to Henderson in 1942, in recognition of US Senator Charles Belknap Henderson. By 1954, according to US census figures, Henderson, which is located approximately sixteen miles southeast of modern Las Vegas, became America's fastest-growing city.

African Americans were not allowed to reside in the Strip area, so they had to live west of the Union Pacific tracks in West Las Vegas, which would come to be known as Westside. As Sarann recalled, "Whenever it rained, mud would be up to your ankles." A severe housing shortage limited their living options even more. Existing houses were small, with no water or sewage, because banks would not loan money to blacks. Many residents had big cars, because they could afford these without financial assistance, but not a big house. Sarann's family lived in various places for a few years until her father used his carpentry skills to build them their own home.

Few jobs were available for black women, so Sarann went to Los Angeles to attend business school. Leaving Las Vegas also allowed her to get away from her husband, who had become abusive. They eventually divorced. Even with her new skills, Sarann could not get an office position in Las Vegas, so she took a job in the Cotton Club in Westside as a Keno (game similar to lotto) writer. Her duties, which included taking customers' bets and marked tickets, running the game, and then paying off the winner, only earned her $4.50 daily, but tips helped her support her family. The fact that she didn't drink, smoke, or gamble also bolstered her financial status.

To expand her knowledge of various forms of gambling, Sarann learned how to deal the card game "21" with help from another employee. She also tried marriage again, the second of several more short-lived ventures, this time with William "Bill" Scruggs, a recently discharged serviceman who worked as a substitute teacher.

When he couldn't find a full-time position, the two decided to move to Hawthorne, about three hundred miles northwest of Las Vegas, in 1950. The Hawthorne Naval Ammunition Depot was hiring, so prospects of her husband finding a job were good. Sarann got a job too—running a club of her own.

Like Las Vegas, Hawthorne was segregated. But the white owner of the Lincoln Bar offered to let Sarann buy it for $600. She borrowed the money from her parents and obtained a gaming license, giving her the distinction of being the first black woman to acquire a nonrestricted gaming license. She touted, "As far as the national records indicate, I was the first African-American female to receive a nonrestricted gaming license in the world in the 1950s. Gaming was not going on in any other places, other than in Nassau in the Bahamas, but women were not allowed to gamble there." She opened the establishment as the Tonga Club in November. It was the only integrated business in Hawthorne. Sarann's tasty barbeque sauce brought many people back to eat, drink, and gamble, and the business was successful for seven years.

In Hawthorne, Sarann began participating in organizations. She was active in the Order of the Eastern Star, an auxiliary group for women associated with the Masons. She served as president of the Mineral County chapter of the NAACP for two terms, and under her efforts for change, it was noted that "things started moving." The group worked to end segregation on buses, playgrounds, and recreation halls.

Sarann returned to Las Vegas in 1957, when the Naval Ammunition Depot downsized and her husband lost his job. She started working at the El Morocco. When it closed after a year, she moved to the Louisiana Club, which had a brown pelican—that state's official bird—pictured on its gaming chips, and then to the Town Tavern, which was known as a hot spot in Westside. Louis Armstrong, a well-known American trumpeter and influential jazz figure, would often stop by. Sarann was working here when the city passed a resolution to prohibit female dealers in 1958, based on the belief that female dealers enticed men to gamble more, thereby upsetting family stability.

At the age of thirty-eight, when most people's lives begin to stabilize, hers began a period of uncertainty. She obtained a job in a black casino in Reno, where women could still deal, but only stayed a few months because she missed her children. Sarann trained at the Las Vegas Beauty College, but later decided it was not a job she wanted. However, she must have retained the knowledge because she was known throughout her lifetime for her polished appearance and stylish dress, generally with a hat. Western Airlines gave her a scholarship to attend real estate school, but Sarann also found this was not to her liking.

The following year, Sarann obtained a job at a dry cleaner and ultimately ended up running it as Sarann's Cleaners. To expand her business, she started selling clothes at the same location. While on a business trip to Los Angeles, a tire on her car blew and the accident resulted in bad injuries to her legs. She sold the cleaning business and opened the Playhouse Lounge with a friend in 1969, on the site of the old Cotton Club. Unable to obtain a gaming license, Sarann had to rely on other tactics in order to attract customers: a fancy decor of marble-topped tables paired with hot-pink furniture, and black entertainers who had scheduled shows on the Strip and were willing to drop by and perform. The Playhouse Lounge only lasted about a year.

The NAACP was still working to get African Americans into gaming positions on the Strip. Jerry's Nugget Casino agreed to hire a black dealer if a qualified person could be found. Enter Sarann. Although she figured this position would be short-lived, she remained there for seven years. She met Joe Lee Preddy while working there. Born in Arkansas in 1935, he was much younger, but Sarann always appreciated that he supported her ideas. Having divorced her second husband and married and divorced two more times, Joe became her fifth husband when they wed on December 10, 1978.

Sarann made history again in 1979. With the support of the NAACP, she ran for a seat on the Las Vegas City Council and was the first black woman to win a primary election. Although the news media originally announced that she had won the general election, it was later determined that she lost by just seventy-two votes. Undeterred by this political loss, Sarann ran for Clark County Commissioner in 1988. She did not win, but these experiences in politics convinced her of the importance of working for African American candidates and promoting issues that affected the black community. She joined the League of Women Voters of Nevada and worked to create the Las Vegas Barbara Jordan Democratic Club. Sarann was also instrumental in founding the Nevada Black Chamber of Commerce, which was later renamed the Urban Chamber of Commerce to embrace inclusiveness. She continued to work with the NAACP, serving on their Executive Board and organizing their local Women's Auxiliary.

After her first political foray, Sarann got back into the business world. She and Joe bought a tavern on Owens Street in Westside, which they renamed Sarann's Supper Club. The kitchen space was limited and remodeling was too expensive, so Sarann turned it into a casino called the People's Choice. Poker, slots, and "21" kept her customers entertained. She ran this for around seven years before she started her quest to resurrect the Moulin Rouge.

Sarann's "never-say-'no' policy" also led her to organize many community activities. She helped create the Las Vegas Black Historical Society and Pioneer Trail, a six-mile excursion that was designed to highlight thirty historic sites in West Las Vegas, including the Moulin Rouge. It is still in existence with sixteen trail markers, and can be completed on foot or via automobile. In 1993, she also worked on the formation of the Alpha Rho chapter of the Gamma Phi Delta Sorority, the first organization for African American businesswomen in Las Vegas.

The four-story Sarann Knight Apartment Complex opened in 2009. Developer Frank Hawkins named it in her honor because she was a pioneer in creating opportunities in the Westside community and he was building innovative, energy efficient units to promote growth in the same area. Other phases of buildings, specifically for senior citizens, were added later. With its proximity to Jackson Street, tenants who live there are close to the area where Sarann spent many hours.

In 2010, Sarann got to wear a special hat. At the age of ninety, she received an honorary doctoral degree from the University of Nevada, Las Vegas (UNLV) for her contributions to the Las Vegas area and the entire state of Nevada. The only other African-American woman to be honored in this manner was long-time Vegas performer Diana Ross in 1984. In his presentation of the degree, UNLV President Dr. Neal Smatresk commented: "Sarann Knight Preddy, it is safe to say that without your unyielding and enduring effort in the Las Vegas business community over the past sixty years, many of the opportunities that await this, one of UNLV's most diverse graduating classes, may not have been available."

In 2011, Sarann was presented the Racial Harmony Hall of Fame Lifetime Achievement "Living Legend" Award. That same year, she was asked to be a co-marshal for the 2011 Martin Luther King Parade in Las Vegas. In an interview with the *Las Vegas Review-Journal* about this event and her achievements, she noted: "I feel proud. Sometimes I think, 'How did I do all of those things?' Then I think, 'I'm 90 years old. I had to do something. I wouldn't know what to do with myself if I wasn't busy.'"

Sarann was honored by many organizations, and due to the media coverage she received for these awards, people often recognized her when she was out in public. She cherished one recognition the most— being named an Ambassador for Peace by the Women's Federation of World Peace—because its focus was peace, not prejudice.

Sarann's life story was featured in two documentaries: the 2012 film *The Gaming Queen* and a segment of the 2014 series *MAKERS: Women in Nevada History*, which was created through the efforts of

UNLV's Women's Research Institute in conjunction with Public Broadcasting Service Las Vegas.

After a prolonged illness and hospitalization, Sarann died at the age of ninety-four on December 22, 2014. A memorial celebration was held on New Year's Eve at Second Baptist Church, her place of worship since her initial move to Las Vegas. Because her husband, Joe, had died on July 9, 1999, from heart failure at age sixty-three, and three of her children preceded her in death, her son James made sure her autobiography, *72 Years in Las Vegas*, reached publication in 2015.

Sarann Knight Preddy will be remembered for her extensive and multifaceted contributions to the African American community in Las Vegas. City Councilman Ricki Barlow called her "a pillar of Las Vegas history" because she helped move the city beyond its discriminatory early days to what it is today—an international travel destination where people of all races enjoy the many activities the city has to offer. Perhaps the secret behind her accomplishments was her motto: "Always treat people the way you want to be treated." Or it may have been the elegant way she spoke and quietly handled situations. She had, as the NAACP said in its tribute to her, a "peaceful, straight-talking, warrior-woman spirit."

Geneva Smith Douglas. —Geneva Douglas Papers [UNRS-P1997-16-00001],
University Libraries, Special Collections Department, University of Nevada, Reno

13

GENEVA ANN SMITH DOUGLAS
(1932–1993)

Ka-Boom! She Relieved Public Fears as Atomic Bombs Exploded

Over forty-two million visitors flock to Las Vegas every year for continuous gambling, food prepared by world-famous chefs, and spectacular stage shows in over one hundred casinos. The city was much different in 1950, however, when fewer than twenty-five thousand people lived within its boundaries and there were only three hotel casinos (the El Rancho Vegas, the Last Frontier, and the Flamingo), all on US 91 outside the city limits. The section of road with these casinos became known as "the Strip," patterning itself after Los Angeles's glitzy Sunset Strip of the 1930s and 1940s. People could also gamble at the smaller gaming parlors that prospered on Fremont Street, a downtown area that earned the name "Glitter Gulch" due to the many lights that followed the installation of the first neon light in 1927.

Throughout the 1950s, more hotel casino complexes sprang up on the Strip and people started to see that Las Vegas offered more than gambling. Big name entertainment, such as singers Frank Sinatra and Peggy Lee and comedian Milton Berle, also drew tourists. One study of the history of the city noted: "The arrival of so much talent in Las Vegas attracted the attention of major magazines and newspapers. In 1953, the *Wall Street Journal, New York Times, Los Angeles Times,*

Variety, Saturday Evening Post, Life, Look, and *Time,* among dozens of periodicals, published articles that noted the explosion of celebrities appearing in the showrooms."

The city, always looking for new ways to attract visitors, found an unlikely source to promote tourism thanks to the federal government's reaction to global tensions. The Nevada Proving Ground—which later became the Nevada Test Site and today is officially called the Nevada National Security Site—started aboveground detonations of atomic bombs in 1951. Although they were located about sixty-five miles northwest of Las Vegas, the first tests, conducted between January 27 and February 6, 1951, shattered several store windows in the city. One enterprising merchant put out a barrel of broken glass in front of his store with the sign, "Atomic Bomb Souvenirs—Free." They were gone in less than an hour.

The actions of the Atomic Energy Commission gained nationwide recognition on April 22, 1952, when an explosion was broadcast to the public on a rapidly expanding new medium—television. Reporters and cameramen were given security clearances to watch the blasts from "News Nob," a small hill ten miles from the blast site. Although dark glasses were required, imagine how intense the thermal heat and shock waves must have been for them, considering that people hundreds of miles away could see and hear the blast. The photographs and commentary amazed Americans. An archival newsreel featuring a well-known journalist of the time describes one such event: "This is Walter Cronkite and this is Newsman's Nob. Some seventy-five miles north of Las Vegas, Nevada, the bomb will be exploded from a tower three hundred feet high and this time some thousand troops will be in trenches only some two miles from the tower where the atomic device goes off."

These explosions touched off the craze for all things "atomic" that swept across the nation. Due to its proximity to the tests, Las Vegas became the epicenter of the fad. It advertised itself as "Up and Atom City," and the Chamber of Commerce provided calendars

Atomic bomb blast at Frenchman's Flats, Nevada. Photographed from vantage point high atop Mt. Charleston, near Las Vegas. —Eva Bertrand Adams Photograph Collection, University Libraries, Special Collections Department [UNRS-P1993-03-1000], University of Nevada, Reno

with detonation times and the best spots for watching the resulting mushroom clouds.

Some casinos started offering "atomic cocktails," a potent mixture of equal parts vodka, brandy, and champagne along with a splash of sherry, served in heat-resistant, shatterproof glasses. Twenty-one-year-old Elvis Presley, who debuted in Las Vegas at the New Frontier Hotel in 1956, was billed as "The Atomic Powered Singer." In 1957, at the beauty pageant for Miss Atomic Bomb, contestants had fluffy cotton mushroom clouds pinned to their swimsuits and were said to glow with "loveliness instead of deadly atomic particles." Tourists could purchase "atomic box lunches" and enjoy a picnic as close to ground zero as the government would permit. Women were willing to pay $75 (equivalent to about $685 today) for the "Atomic Hairdo," where their hair was pulled over a mushroom-shaped wire form and sprinkled with silver glitter. They wore this to "Dawn Bomb Parties," where people ate and danced to songs such as the "Atomic Boogie" and "Radioactive Mama" until the night sky exploded with light from a nuclear test.

Binion's Horseshoe was one of the first "carpet joints" on Fremont Street, meaning the casino floors were covered with carpet rather than sawdust. Now called Binion's Gambling Hall & Hotel, the original owner, Benny Binion, said, "The best thing to happen to Vegas was the Atomic Bomb." Clark County, where Las Vegas is located, must have agreed, because in the 1950s they incorporated a mushroom cloud into the official county seal that remained until 1962.

Children practiced "duck and cover" drills in school after watching a movie from the US Federal Civil Defense Administration starring Bert the Turtle, who demonstrated the safety technique by hiding in his shell. Children could obtain gumballs from rocket-shaped dispensers and dared each other to eat the spicy, cinnamon-flavored candy called the Atomic Fireball.

In 1956, Walt Disney published a children's book called *Our Friend the Atom*. Written by physicist Heinz Haber, a professor at the

University of Southern California, the 165-page book discussed the positive and negative aspects of atomic power and emphasized its uses for the "welfare of all mankind." As Walt Disney stated in the introduction: "Atomic science began as positive, creative thought. It has created modern science with its many benefits for mankind. In this sense our book tries to make it clear to you that we can indeed look upon the atom as our friend."

In 1963, the Atomic Energy Commission collaborated with the Boy Scouts of America to create the Atomic Energy merit badge. To earn it, boys could select from a variety of possible projects such as building an electroscope to detect the amount of electrical charge in the body, building a model of a reactor to simulate a controlled nuclear reaction, or constructing a cloud chamber to detect charged particles like those in radiation. By 1970, fifteen thousand scouts had earned this badge. In 2005, the Atomic Energy merit badge was renamed Nuclear Science merit badge but maintained similar criteria to its predecessor.

Young and old alike were caught up in the atomic pop culture obsession. The cover of the 1953 Las Vegas High School yearbook included a mushroom cloud, and teen couples swooned when rhythm and blues singer Little Caesar professed: "Boom! Something exploded down inside / And rushed teardrops to my eyes / Oh, yes, I have that funny feeling / I guess it's my atomic love, for you."

For twelve years, from 1951 to 1963, an average of one bomb every three weeks was detonated—235 bombs total. Of course, all Americans were aware that the bombs dropped on Hiroshima and Nagasaki caused devastation and motivated Japan to surrender, which ended World War II. Therefore, some Las Vegas citizens were concerned about the potential danger of the atomic tests conducted so close to their city and went so far as to make children wear military-style identification tags "just in case."

But the Atomic Energy Commission stressed to the American public the need to keep testing, citing the danger of communism and the Cold War with the United Soviet Socialist Republic. They downplayed the hazards of radioactive fallout, stating that there would be little risk to Las Vegas. Details were outlined in a green pamphlet called "Atomic Tests in Nevada" which stated: "findings have confirmed that Nevada test fallout has not caused illness or injured the health of anyone living near the test site." Thirty thousand copies of this brochure were distributed to people in the areas around the test site. The public was also reassured that they would be safe if they stayed indoors until the fallout had stopped, or—if caught outdoors—they were instructed to "bathe, wash hair, dust clothes, clean shoes." Although the 1963 signing of the Limited Test Ban Treaty banned all aboveground nuclear tests, underground tests continued until 1992.

A sense of patriotism, an increase in business and revenue from the influx of government employees involved in the testing program, and demand from tourists who wanted to experience nuclear blasts helped alleviate any misgivings held by the city's residents. Another factor was the competent government liaison between the nuclear industry and the people of Nevada—Geneva Ann Smith Douglas. Being a radiation biologist was an unusual career for a woman and completely beyond the boundaries of what was considered a proper occupation for a woman at the time. Men dominated the scientific fields, yet here was Geneva, an expert in radiation.

—•••—

Although Geneva is an unusual name today, it was popular in the early part of the twentieth century, perhaps because Geneva, Switzerland, became the headquarters of the League of Nations in 1920. Formed after World War I, the mission of the league was to provide a venue for resolving international issues and maintaining world peace. The city hosted multinational conventions where the treatment of soldiers and civilians during wars was discussed. International treaties, such as the 1925 Geneva Protocol that prohibited the use of chemical and biological weapons in war, were signed there. The League of Nations formally dissolved on April 18, 1946, and transferred its mission to the United Nations, an organization that still exists with headquarters in New York City. Although the United States never joined the League of Nations, its activities and the outcomes of the world meetings were widely publicized in the United States.

So when James Raymond and Ella Elizabeth (Novak) Smith had a baby on April 24, 1932, in Gloucester, Massachusetts, she was named Geneva Ann Smith. Her mother died seven days later. In October 1933, James married Edna Louise Brannon, a graduate of Miss Farmer's School of Cookery in Boston and proprietor of the Driftwood Tea Room, a business she started in 1929. Geneva's father was the owner of a lumber and hardware store, a family business started in 1874 in the small, coastal town of Rockport, Massachusetts. Geneva's parents later purchased Driftwood Farm, the name of a huge house that looked over Whale Cove and the spot on the beach where French explorer Samuel de Champlain stepped ashore on July 16, 1605—reportedly the first white man in this part of Massachusetts. The promontory became known as the Cape of Islands.

By 1937, Geneva's stepmother was running Driftwood Farm as a guesthouse, probably because of economic difficulties during the Great Depression, which lasted from 1929 to 1939. Geneva's dad died suddenly, at age fifty-nine, on December 27, 1947. That New Year's holiday was sad for Geneva and her half sister Susan, born in 1935, and half brother Raymond, born in 1938. Edna took over the operation of the lumber and hardware business at that point.

After graduating from Rockport High School, Geneva attended Colby College, a small coed liberal arts institution in Waterville, Maine, where she participated in the student theater club, called the Powder and Wig, and the Life Science Colloquium. The 1954 *Oracle* yearbook shows she was a member of the Phi Beta Kappa honor society, a distinction reserved for only the most outstanding students.

After graduating with cum laude honors, Geneva continued her education at Mount Holyoke College, a liberal arts college for women in South Hadley, Massachusetts, where she worked as a graduate assistant in the Physiology (the study of living matter including parts of the human body) Department and received her graduate degree in 1956.

Geneva went on to do more postgraduate work in physiology, radiation biology, and health physics at the Marine Biology Laboratory at Woods Hole, Massachusetts, and at the University of Rochester in New York, where she also worked as a research associate studying the metabolism of nuclear fission products for the Atomic Energy Project. This program was designed to continue the research of the World War II Manhattan Project, which had produced the first atomic weapons. It also trained people in how to employ atomic energy for peaceful purposes. Geneva stayed in this job until 1959.

That year, national radiological health requirements were established, and the Southwestern Radiological Health Laboratory (SWRHL) was created in Las Vegas as part of the US Public Health Service. SWRHL served as the main facility for radiological research and review in all of the western states. Similar to what was happening at the University of Rochester, SWRHL became the training agency for people working in the atomic energy field in states west of the Mississippi River as well as in Alaska and Hawaii.

Geneva was hired as a radiation biologist for SWRHL, which by the 1980s became known as the Environmental Monitoring Systems Laboratory of Las Vegas (EMSL-LV). She became the liaison between the nuclear industry and the local community under dual positions as the Public Affairs Director for the Public Health Service and Public Information Director for the US Environmental Protection Agency (EPA). Much of her time was spent preparing informational news releases and fact sheets about nuclear weapons. Through slideshows and talks to community groups, she explained nuclear testing and the federal program to monitor its effects on the environment. She also conducted tours for visitors at the Nevada Test Site.

Geneva met Richard Lee Douglas in Las Vegas, where he worked for the Bioenvironmental Research Program of SWRHL. Like Geneva, he authored scientific papers such as "Status of the Nevada Test Site Experimental Farm" (January 1966) and was the coauthor of the 1971 publication *Transport Through the Air-Forage-Cow-Milk System Using an Aerosol Mist (Project Rainout)*. He later moved to the EPA as a safety officer in the Las Vegas Office of Radiation Programs. An Indiana native, born on December 30, 1937, in Crawfordsville, he graduated from Purdue University in 1959. He and Geneva married on December 28, 1963. They bought a home in Las Vegas on a half-acre lot in the desert. As much as possible, Geneva and Richard would spend May through October near her family in Rockport, Massachusetts, and November through April at their home in Las Vegas.

Following the accident at the Three Mile Island Nuclear Generating Station in Dauphin County, Pennsylvania, on March 28, 1979, Geneva supervised the emergency response crew that vented krypton, a radioactive gas, during the cleanup in July 1980. Krypton is produced by the splitting of uranium and plutonium in nuclear reactors. That same year, federal documents unclassified by President Jimmy Carter showed that radioactive material from the atomic bomb explosions in Nevada in the 1950s had drifted over the Los Angeles area. Geneva was quoted in a national news article stating that "the incident probably was not hazardous because the peak amount represented a portion of 1 roentgen." Scientists felt that a safe radiation dose for atomic workers was 5 roentgens (also spelled röntgens) during a one-year period, although this was later dropped to 2.5 roentgens. The unit measurement of radiation was named for its discoverer, Wilhelm Conrad Röntgen.

Eventually, Geneva decided she wanted to do more than just speak, write, and consult on matters related to nuclear energy.

When she became Program Operations Manager of EMSL-LV, she designed an off-site program that established radiation-monitoring stations in local communities. The stations were operated on a daily basis by residents—such as high school science teachers—who had some scientific expertise. In addition, an EPA monitor checked each station weekly. Geneva also participated in the town hall meetings that were held throughout 1982 to get community feedback and to explain the history of off-site radiation monitoring while listening to and alleviating any fears about the nuclear testing program. She outlined the program in her technical report of May 1983 for the US Department of Energy: *A Community Monitoring Program Surrounding the Nevada Test Site: One Year of Experience.* Geneva had fifteen such academic publications. She was the EPA nominee for the Congressional Award for Exemplary Service in 1983.

Geneva was also a participant in and evaluator for the field exercises of the Federal Radiological Emergency Response Plan (FRERP). The first test was at the St. Lucie Nuclear Power Plant in Florida in March 1984; there was another one in June 1987 at the Nuclear Power Plant in Zion, Illinois. She acted as the EPA spokesperson after accidental releases of radioactivity occurred in the United States and China, and she testified before the US Congress about the basics of nuclear testing, levels of radiation exposure, and the disposal of nuclear waste in storage repositories.

Geneva worked for the EPA until 1985, and that year she was awarded the Public Health Service Meritorious Service Medal. Even after retirement, she continued to act as a tour guide at the Nevada Test Site. As she led people around in 1989, remnants of the bleachers from "News Nob" (where reporters watched the atmospheric tests of the 1950s) were still visible. By special appointment, she also continued to work for the EPA as a consultant.

Geneva was active for many years in the Soroptimist International of Greater Las Vegas, a local chapter of a large service organization for women. Originally chartered in 1950 as Soroptimist International of Las Vegas–Paradise Valley, the name was changed in 1976 and Geneva was a charter member of the new group, whose business and professional female members strived to improve the lives of women and girls, both internationally and in their local communities. Between 1968 and 1980, she held most of the officer positions, including two terms as president from 1976 to 1978.

Geneva was elected governor of the Sierra Nevada Region in 1980, where she monitored almost fifty Soroptimist clubs in Nevada and California until 1982. Moving to the international level, she became the environmental advisor for a group of clubs in twenty countries called Soroptimist International of the Americas, a position she held from 1982 to 1984. Attending the International Soroptomist Convention of 1983 in Istanbul, Turkey, she was appointed as a representative to the eighty-nation Long Range Planning Group. In 1987, she became the international programme liaison. Not only did she coordinate international service programs in economic and social development, education, and human rights, but she also created a roster of members with special expertise who could act as consultants when needed. For this position, she traveled to Norway, Australia, and New Zealand, as well as other countries, and documented her travels through slides. Geneva remained in this role until 1991.

The Nevada Nuclear Waste Study Committee, which is now known as the Study Committee, was a nonprofit organization established in 1984 to generate citizen support for a high-level radioactive waste repository at Yucca Mountain in Nye County, about one hundred miles northwest of Las Vegas. A full-page ad by the group in the *Reno Gazette-Journal* on August 16, 1988, outlined their objectives for this facility:

> 1. Continued scientific study of the repository should proceed, monitored by both the newly created Technical Review Board, made up of scientists nominated by the National Academy of Sciences, and the State of Nevada.

2. State and local officials should take positive and responsible action to obtain all economic benefits possible under the law that established the repository program.

A huge list of supporters' names is included, and Geneva's name appears because she was a member of the steering committee. The site acted as a permanent nuclear waste storage facility until 2010, when it was no longer deemed "a workable option," although efforts started in 2017 to reopen the site.

Governor Richard Bryan established the Governor's Advisory Committee on Volunteerism in 1986 and selected Geneva as the chairperson. The committee's goals were to assist the Nevada Office of Volunteerism by recruiting volunteer leaders and organizing ser- vice activities within the state. In 1987, under Geneva's guidance, the group held the Nevada Volunteer Leadership Conference, the first statewide conference to focus on volunteerism. It was considered a huge success, with over 150 business and service organizations as well as representatives from forty-five government agencies at the local, state, and federal level in attendance.

Geneva's concern for environmental protection also led her to the Friends of Nevada Wilderness, a group that still exists today and whose mission is "preserving all qualified Nevada public lands as wilderness, protecting all present and potential wilderness from ongoing threats, informing the public about the values of and need for wilderness, and restoring and improving the management of wild lands." As chairperson from 1986 to 1987, Geneva was responsible for preparing press releases and providing congressional testimony relating to the safeguarding of wilderness terrain. She was also instrumental in obtaining support for the establishment of Great Basin National Park in 1986. Located in White Pine County, close to the town of Baker and the Utah border, visitors can explore groves of ancient bristlecone pine trees and the underground beauty of the Lehman Caves, originally protected as a National Monument in 1922.

Geneva died on January 30, 1993, at age sixty in Las Vegas. After a memorial service in that city, she was buried in her family's plot at the Beech Grove Cemetery in Rockport. Another memorial service was held on February 21 at the Rockport Congregational Church, as reported in the *Gloucester Daily Times*.

Nevada still touts its history with the atomic bomb. Although the 2002 attempt to get a charitable license plate with a mushroom cloud design failed, due to strong feelings about the safety of the Yucca Mountain nuclear waste repository, plates with the outline of the Nevada Test Site and the atomic symbol became available from the Nevada Department of Motor Vehicles in 2017. While the general public is much more aware of the dangers of nuclear energy today, institutions such as the National Atomic Testing Museum in Las Vegas and the monthly, heavily booked tours to the Nevada National Security Site continue to provide insights into the attitudes of the early days of atomic testing, when Geneva started her work in the field.

Her early message to the people of Nevada was the one promoted by the government, as in this 1955 report: "The American people can be assured that the rigorous safeguards which govern the tests are designed to prevent injury to the people of any community or city . . . . Rigid precautions are taken to hold the fallout from Nevada test shots to an absolute minimum." But Geneva was a scientist and that meant she viewed her field objectively. She did her own research through the off-site radiation-monitoring program she developed and wrote about her findings. Her concern for the environment also originated from her knowledge of nuclear energy.

It was uncommon for women in her era to work in science, technology, engineering, and mathematical fields, but Geneva bravely and directly faced opponents of nuclear energy and women's rights during her career. Seeing herself as a role model for other women, she participated passionately in the Soroptomist organization and urged others to volunteer their time and expertise. She wanted to leave a better state for future generations. Geneva's contributions to Nevada are not widely known today. Her legacy seems to echo that of Geneva, Nevada, which was established in 1863 as a prosperous mining town but is now a ghost town. Both were bold and adventurous in their era, but their contributions to Nevada have sadly been lost over time.

14

MARCIA DE BRAGA
(1937–2010)

Ranching, Rodeo, and Rural Nevada Were Her Passions

Marcia de Braga loved children. She had four of her own, but the loss of a baby daughter was a lasting and painful memory. In April 2000, when she heard about the above-average number of children living in Fallon who were contracting the life-threatening disease of leukemia, she was determined to get to the bottom of the problem. Fallon is situated in Churchill County in northwestern Nevada and is part of the Assembly District No. 35 that Marcia represented in the state legislature from 1993 to 2001. She had a professional as well as personal reason to get involved.

Fallon, the designated county seat, is a small town located in the high desert about an hour east of Reno. In the 2010 US Census, around eighty-six hundred people lived in the town, and even less were there between 1995 and 2002, when sixteen children were diagnosed with acute lymphoblastic leukemia (ALL), a cancer that affects the blood and bone marrow. ALL requires immediate treatment because it rapidly produces abnormal white blood cells that prohibit the body from fighting infection. ALL is the most common form of childhood leukemia.

When Marcia learned about the cluster of cases in Fallon, she requested that the Nevada State Health Division of the Nevada

Marcia de Braga. —Courtesy of the Nevada State Assembly

Department of Health and Human Services investigate. Health officials started interviewing the affected families in June, but the results were disappointing. No causal factor was pinpointed.

Marcia did not give up. In February 2001, she put forth a bill requesting $1 million for environmental testing. The bill did not pass, but Marcia continued her quest and finally got federal attention. At a Congressional Field Hearing held at the Fallon Convention Center on April 12, 2001, she shared her motivation: "Why do I feel so strongly that we have a responsibility to move forward in every way possible? Because this is about children—children whose lives have been turned upside down by something terrible that's beyond their control. This is about a beautiful, smiling little girl whose hair is gone. This is about a promising young athlete whose energy now only lasts for minutes. This is about a teenager whose HMO won't pay for a bone marrow transplant." Marcia was joined at this gathering by US Senators Harry Reid of Nevada and Hillary Rodham Clinton of New York, who were members of the Senate Environment and Public Works Committee, as well as Nevada Governor Kenny Guinn. Senator Reid described the purpose for the meeting: "The State of Nevada, the City of Fallon, the US Navy, the Centers for Disease Control and others are already working on this important issue, and enhanced coordination is essential to maximize this effort. We also will explore the availability of additional federal resources and hear from local and state officials about remaining community needs."

This event provided the motivation to pull together a committee of outside experts who recommended a systematic analysis of all the contaminants to which the families with affected children could have been exposed. Two federal agencies were recommended: the US Centers for Disease Control and Prevention (CDC) and the Agency for Toxic Substances and Disease Registries. An intensive investigation ensued. Carol Rubin, who headed the CDC investigation, stated: "As researchers, we invested an extraordinary amount of time and effort and planning and really wanted to find an explanation."

First, they explored jet fuel fumes from Naval Air Station Fallon, which is located southeast of the town. The Naval Fighter Weapons School (more colloquially known as Top Gun) was moved there in 1996 from Miramar Naval Air Station in San Diego, California. The flight school used approximately thirty-four million gallons of jet fuel annually. The fuel—made up of over two hundred chemicals, including benzene, a substance known to cause cancer in humans— was found in a pipeline under the playground at the local elementary school. A leak was suspected but never found. Navy jets also sometimes dumped fuel over the outskirts of the town before landing, and the wind blew droplets of this contaminated liquid around the area.

Second, they found arsenic in the town's drinking water, in quantities ten times higher than federal standards. The town resisted addressing this costly problem. Marcia noted: "I don't know if they're in denial, or firmly believe that since Grandpa Jones drank it all his life it's not a serious problem. But they need to bite the bullet." In 2003, construction of a new water treatment facility was started due to Marcia's continued efforts. The federal government contributed $100,000 to provide bottled water to the community until the plant was completed. Senator Harry Reid, who announced the funding, remarked, "Marcia de Braga and the parents just wouldn't give up. They wouldn't back down in their efforts to help these children. Marcia wouldn't quit pushing."

Third, they explored pesticides as a possible cause. The land around Fallon is used for agriculture, and the many farms raise vegetables, herbs, and fruit. Around 60 percent of all agricultural products grown in Nevada come from the area, and it has been labeled the "Oasis of Nevada" and "Nevada's Salad Bowl." Alfalfa for livestock feed is also a major crop. Local farmers use pesticides on their fields, and the sick children lived mostly in the agriculture and pasture region of Churchill County, outside of the "developed" area of Fallon. But no definite proof could be found to link pesticides to the cancer outbreak.

Tungsten was also considered as a possible disease source because a processing plant was located next to the elementary school in the town. But again, tests were inconclusive. Marcia was dismayed, and as she told the *Reno Gazette-Journal* in August 2002, "We've got laboratory scientists, but what we need is a Columbo, a relentless detective with imagination. This isn't a statistical problem. There are flesh-and-blood children involved." Although the most intensive investigation ever conducted into a cancer cluster occurred, no single cause was ever isolated. The official investigation closed in 2004, although a few individual studies are still active. The area did not have another ALL patient until 2012, eleven years after the last reported in 2001.

Marcia's tireless effort to investigate and promote new research into the causes of childhood leukemia is in itself noteworthy, but it was just one of many accomplishments she achieved in working for the people of Nevada.

———•••———

Marcia Dune Smith was born on April 14, 1937, in Los Angeles, California, to Elden and Zona Dee (Peterson) Smith. Her father was reportedly a lineal descendent of Joseph Smith, the founder of the Mormon religion and the Church of Jesus Christ of Latter-day Saints. He worked as an aircraft painter for the Lockheed Corporation. Elden reportedly went out to purchase cigarettes one day and abandoned the family when Marcia was around seven years old. Zona fended off unkind comments that suggested she had driven off her husband, and Marcia felt sorry for her mother.

Left to raise three daughters (Marcia had two sisters, Kaaren and Suzanne), her mother moved them to Salt Lake City, Utah, to live with her mother. They returned to Zona's home state of Idaho, where they lived in a one-room cabin in Sugar City, and the girls resumed their schooling. Marcia was in fourth grade. The wood-burning stove did little to alleviate the biting winter cold felt so deeply by the girls, who were accustomed to mild southern California weather. Zona acquired certification as a cosmetician and opened up a beauty shop near where they lived.

She met a returning World War II soldier named Bernell R. Murdock, who had been born in Rexburg, Idaho, on October 19, 1920. The brown-haired, brown-eyed Marine Corps veteran charmed Zona, and on March 19, 1948, the two went to Idaho Falls to be married. The last name of the three girls changed to Murdock when he adopted them. The couple attended Ricks College (named for Marcia's Mormon paternal great-grandfather, Thomas Edwin Ricks) in Rexburg to acquire teaching certification. Zona finished first and got a job in Pocatello, where the family moved in time for Marcia to start sixth grade. Just before Marcia entered eighth grade, Bernell finished his coursework, and they moved to Churchill County in Nevada with both adults taking teaching positions in Stillwater's three-room schoolhouse, which was built in 1918. Zona handled the lower grades and Bernell taught the students in grades five through eight.

Marcia graduated from Stillwater in a class of three students and went on to Churchill County High School in Fallon. She participated in the Girls' Athletic Association, and her cooking and sewing skills were improved in the Future Homemakers of America Club. Her grades made her academically eligible to be an Alpha Lambda member. She was a staff member of the school yearbook, *Lahontan*, in 1954. After a long day at school, she probably visited with friends and drank sodas at the Do-Drop Inn. She loved movies, especially *The Wizard of Oz*, so she acquired many ticket stubs from the Lawana Theater on Maine Street in Fallon. The street name reflected the home state of Warren W. Williams, who bought Mike Fallon's ranch and laid out the west side of the town named for him.

Marcia graduated from high school early, and on February 11, 1955, at age seventeen, she married Lyle N. de Braga, who came from a longtime Churchill County family. He was older and out of school, and they met at a public dance. She appreciated his gentle nature and ability to make her laugh. She always called him "her best friend." They settled on a ranch in Stillwater, where Marcia enjoyed watching the birds and wildlife that frequented the wetlands of the area, including the Stillwater National Wildlife Refuge, established in 1949. Marcia initially knew little about ranching and once noted that on the ranch, she acquiesced to her husband. As she explained, "He said 'The Boss' should be able to tell the difference between hay fields and grain fields. Since the only thing on the farm I could possibly identify was dirt, I was never in the running." But Marcia came to appreciate the ranch lifestyle and was glad her children got to grow up in that environment. Lael Norma arrived first. Francis Gayle was next but only lived a short time. Later, Jaime joined the family, followed by Joe and Mitzi.

As the children got older, Marcia sought new ways to fill her time. She loved playing bridge and baking, especially pies. She often stated: "If heaven were a pie, it would be cherry," part of the lyrics of the Andy Griggs song "If Heaven." As a shy, young girl, she had found newspapers fascinating and developed a love of language. She began writing a "Solemn Column" for the *Lahontan Valley News*. In it, she humorously explored the challenges of daily life in rural Nevada. She was known for making up words if none came to mind for the situation, like a rustic Dr. Seuss. Marcia also was a correspondent for the *Reno Evening Gazette* and *Nevada State Journal*.

In 1964, she published *Dig No Graves* "as a tribute to the history of our locale" from "a person who was born too late to be part of the past but just in time to appreciate it." Through facts and anecdotes, she overviewed one hundred years of Churchill County's past in an entertaining narrative coupled with period photographs. Marcia shared the problems encountered by early settlers as well as the booms and busts of the many mining towns that no longer exist in the county. She exhorted: "We will remember them and let them live!"

Marcia also wrote political poetry, which she sometimes read at Democratic Party gatherings when she served as the chair of the

Churchill County Democratic Party in 2009 and helped organize the Rural Nevada Democratic Caucus. Her final writing was her autobiography, a gift for her family. In it, she described the values she was taught by her mother and stepfather: "tolerance, acceptance, equality for all and compassion." Her prowess with language was once described by a fellow legislator as follows: "The pen and word were her tools. Marcia wielded a pen with more power than a high-powered weapon."

Although adapting to a ranching lifestyle had originally been challenging for her, she did learn to drive a tractor, plow a field, and do other chores needed to maintain a ranch. Marcia became active in the Nevada Cattleman's Association and attended rodeos, 4-H activities, and other school and sports activities in which her children were involved, including events associated with the National High School Rodeo Association. She also served as the secretary for the Nevada State High School Rodeo Association for twenty-one years. It bothered her that young Nevada participants sometimes failed to qualify for the National High School Finals Rodeo by a fraction of a second. Only high school winners in first through fourth place could advance to the finals rodeo at the national level.

Consequently in 1985, she and Lyle, along with friend Rich Lee, cofounded the Nevada International Invitational Rodeo for youth who failed to qualify at the national level. In 1988, the name was changed to the Silver State International Rodeo (SSIR). Marcia acted as the main organizer of SSIR for many years. Starting as a three-day event in Fallon, in 2019, it is slated to run for eight days in Winnemucca. Around five hundred high school participants who end up in fifth through fifteenth place in events that take place all over the West (including Canada) will attend. Occasionally there are entries from eastern states such as Florida and North Carolina, as well as Hawaii, where rodeos are popular, especially on the Big Island.

After being involved in many activities in nonleadership roles, Marcia made a decision: "And I thought, you know what I want to be [is] the top dog in something." So she decided to run for a seat in the Nevada State Assembly and won. She represented Churchill and White Pine Counties as well as some sections of Eureka and Lander Counties (Assembly District No. 35), becoming the voice of the "cow counties" (so-called because of the prevalence of livestock) in 1992. Serving five terms, she worked on many projects, including the effort to investigate the cluster of childhood leukemia cases around Fallon. In her role as an advocate for the children of Nevada, Marcia worked to provide protection for children who lived in a home with parents known to abuse each other. She also promoted legislation that provided funding for the Reno Rodeo and the Nevada High School Rodeo Association. Other major legislation included a bill that prevented the state government from taking Public Employees Retirement System of Nevada funds to plug shortages in other areas.

She chaired the Assembly Committee on Natural Resources, Agriculture, and Mining, helping to craft and pass Assembly Bill 380 in 1999, which settled many water issues in the northern part of the state and compensated people for lost water rights. The *Reno Gazette-Journal* called her "a miracle worker" for helping designate the water usage in the Truckee River that runs from Lake Tahoe to Pyramid Lake. Her maneuverings with the various parties involved with the water bill propelled Marcia to be awarded the 2001 *Good Housekeeping* Women in Government award as a "Nimble Negotiator." One of only ten women in the nation to be selected by US vice presidential candidate Geraldine Ferraro for this honor, Marcia was thrilled when Ferraro also personally presented her with the award.

In 2001, Marcia served Nevada in a different way. Each state may place statues of two individuals in the National Statuary Hall of the US Capitol in Washington DC. But Nevada was one of three states that had recognized only one individual. Former US Senator Pat McCarran had already been placed in the gallery in 1960. Supported by the Nevada Women's History Project, Marcia introduced Assembly Bill 267 in the legislature in 2001. Its purpose was to make the second Nevada statue in honor of Sarah Winnemucca, a Paiute activist who is recognized as the first Indian woman in the United States to publish a book in English (*Life Among the Piutes: Their Wrongs and Claims*, 1883). Initially, Marcia attached $100,000 to the bill to pay for the statue. But that changed, as she explained: "That year there was a tight budget. So I removed the money. I just wanted the bill regardless and hoped we could find a way to raise the money."

The bill passed the assembly and was sent to the Senate Finance Committee. Project members waited impatiently, and it took until the last day of the session for the bill to move out of the committee for the final vote. Perhaps a good omen helped the outcome. Marcia always remembered what Sarah's great-grandniece, Louise Tannheimer, told her about an event that occurred just before that vote was taken: "Louise told me that as she was entering the Capitol Building, she saw an eagle feather lying near its entrance. That feather will bring us good fortune today." It did. Passing with no dissent, the bill was signed by Governor Kenny Guinn on May 29, 2001.

The money for the statue was raised by the Nevada Women's History Project with help from Nevada First Lady Dema Guinn and other organizations. Benjamin Victor sculpted the six-foot-four-inch bronze statue that was dedicated on March 9, 2005. Nevada's Sarah Winnemucca is one of nine statues in the National Statuary Hall that are women.

Although Marcia believed she lost her assembly seat in 2001 due to redistricting, she did not leave politics; she managed the campaigns of other candidates. In 2005, as one of her last efforts, she acted as the rural campaign manager in northern Nevada for Jack Carter, son of US President Jimmy Carter, who challenged Senator John Ensign. Although the former President visited Nevada to bolster his son's chances, Jack lost the race.

Marcia never liked to say "goodbye." She preferred "see you later" or "toodles." But after being diagnosed with cancer and battling the painful disease for some years, she knew it was time for closure. She noted toward the end: "Too many people leave this world before they are even ready to buy their ticket. I am lucky to have been able to say all the things I wanted to say." Marcia died on March 24, 2010, at age seventy-two, surrounded by her family. She was interred at the Churchill County Cemetery in Fallon.

A celebration of life was held at the Fallon Convention Center to accommodate the large number of people who attended. Democratic Nevada politician Rory Reid, the son of US Senator Harry Reid, stated: "Nevada has never had a more dedicated and passionate public servant." Marcia had collaborated on various projects with Rory, and he himself was a gubernatorial candidate that year. Former Governor Robert Miller (1989–1999) recalled that Marcia dealt with issues regardless of their political affiliation and that she understood the needs of rural Nevada: "She felt it was critical for them to be heard. She was a wonderful lady, polite and soft spoken, an ardent proponent." Fallon Mayor Ken Tedford Jr. echoed that sentiment: "When she decided to get into public service in the Legislature, she did a wonderful job for the community and served us well. She worked her hardest." Even Republican assemblyman Pete Goicoechea, who defeated Marcia for her assembly seat in 2002, stated: "I have a tremendous amount of respect for the work she did."

Others have also recognized Marcia over the years. In Fallon, she was honored as the Woman of the Year by the Soroptimist International and named Community Woman of the Year by the American Association of University Women. For her hard work to improve and support agriculture, the Nevada Farm Bureau honored her with the Silver Plow Award. She also received the Nevada High School Rodeo Outstanding Service Award and her affinity with rodeos continues to shine through her grandson Jade Corkill, who has been the world champion Professional Rodeo Cowboys Association team roping heeler for multiple years and acts as a model for Cinch Jeans.

Marcia also received a Truckee Meadows Tomorrow Silver Star Award, given to individuals who have improved the quality of life in that area of the state. The Nevada Women's Lobby recognized her efforts in 1999, and the Nevada State Legislature added Marcia to the Assembly Wall of Distinction in 2011 as one "who demonstrated exceptional service and made significant contributions to the State" as a public servant and private citizen. A memorial scholarship was set up in her name at Churchill County High School after her passing.

In May 2001, Marcia de Braga was the commencement speaker for the graduating class at the Fallon campus of the Western Nevada College. The students appreciated the words of this tough but compassionate woman who made history in the Nevada legislature, recorded history to save the lost voices of their county, and never forgot the friends and neighbors she loved so much in rural Nevada and who loved her in return.

BIBLIOGRAPHY

1. Hannah Keziah Clapp

Baldasano, Mary M. "High Sierra Education: Educator, Philanthropist, Librarian." *Las Vegan Magazine of Las Vegas*. Accessed at http://www.lasvegan.net.

Cassinelli, Dennis. "Stories of Old Nevada: Fence Building at the Old Nevada State Capitol." *Elko Daily Free Press*, March 4, 2017.

Earl, Phillip I. "Nevada—Then and Now: Reno's Kindergarten History." *Pahrump Valley Gazette* 17, March 11, 1999.

Enss, Chris. *Frontier Teachers: Stories of Heroic Women of the Old West*. Guilford, CT: TwoDot, 2008.

Feuer, Margaret. "The Hannah Clapp House—1896." *Palo Alto Stanford Heritage*, July 17, 2015. Accessed at http://www.pastheritage.org.

Geuder, Patricia A., editor. *Pioneer Women of Nevada*. Carson City, NV: Alpha Chi State of the Delta Kappa Gamma Society, International and the Nevada Division of the American Association of University Women, 1976.

Holmes, Kenneth L., editor. *Covered Wagon Women: 1854–1860*. Lincoln, NE: Bison Books, 1987.

Nevada Historical Society. "In Memoriam: Hannah Keziah Clapp." In *Biennial Report of the Nevada Historical Society* 1: 58–60. State Printing Office, 1909.

Ohles, Frederik, Shirley M. Ohles, and John G. Ramsey. *Biographical Dictionary of Modern American Educators*. Westport, CT: Greenwood Press, 1997.

Pistone, Dante. "Carson City Heroine." In *Nevada Official Bicentennial Book*, edited by Stanley W. Paher. Las Vegas: Nevada Publications, 1976.

Pruett, Elizabeth Cornelius. "Kindergarten Goes to the World's Fair: How the World's Fair of 1876 Advanced the Kindergarten Movement in the United States." PhD diss., University of Alabama at Birmingham, 2013.

Totton, Kathryn Dunn. "Hannah Keziah Clapp: The Life and Career of a Pioneer Nevada Educator, 1824–1908." *Nevada Historical Society Quarterly* 20 (Fall 1977): 167–83.

Walton-Buchanan, Holly. "Hannah Keziah Clapp." Nevada Women's History Project, November, 2008. Accessed at http://www.unr.edu/nwhp.

"Women's History Month: Hannah Keziah Clapp, Education Trailblazer." Guest: Eileen Cohen. Nevada Public Radio, April 1, 2011. Accessed at http://www.knpr.org.

Zanjani, Sally. *Devils Will Reign: How Nevada Began*. Reno: University of Nevada Press, 2007.

2. Sarah Winnemucca Hopkins

Canfield, Gae Whitney. *Sarah Winnemucca of the Northern Paiutes*. Norman: University of Oklahoma Press, 1983.

Chartier, JoAnn, and Chris Enss. *She Wore a Yellow Ribbon: Women Soldiers and Patriots of the Western Frontier*. Guilford, CT: TwoDot, 2004.

Cleere, Jan. *More Than Petticoats: Remarkable Nevada Women*. Guilford, CT: TwoDot, 2005.

Enss, Chris. *Tales Behind the Tombstones: The Deaths and Burials of the Old West's Most Nefarious Outlaws, Notorious Women, and Celebrated Lawmen*. Guilford, CT: TwoDot, 2007.

Ford, Victoria, and Janet E. White. "Sarah Winnemucca." In *Skirts That Swept the Desert Floor*, edited by M. A. Duval. Las Vegas: Stephens Press, 2006.

Furbee, Mary Rodd. *Outrageous Women of the American Frontier*. New York: Wiley, 2002.

Hopkins, Sarah W. *Life among the Piutes: Their Wrongs and Claims*. New York: G. P. Putnam's Sons, 1883. Reprinted in 1994 by the University of Nevada Press.

"Hopkins, Sarah W." Obituary. *New York Times*, October 27, 1891.

Hulse, James W. *The Silver State*, 2nd ed. Reno: University of Nevada Press, 1998.

Mahon, Elizabeth Kerri. *Scandalous Women: The Lives and Loves of History's Most Notorious Women*. New York: Perigee Trade, 2011.

Miller, Brandon Marie. *Women of the Frontier: 16 Tales of Trailblazing Homesteaders, Entrepreneurs, and Rabble-Rousers*. Chicago Review Press, 2013.

Morrison, Dorothy Nafus. *Chief Sarah: Sarah Winnemucca's Fight for Indian Rights*. Oregon Historical Society, 1991.

Rosinsky, Natalie M. *Sarah Winnemucca: Scout, Activist, and Teacher*. Mankato, MN: Compass Point Books, 2006.

Sorisio, Carolyn, and Cari M. Carpenter, editors. *The Newspaper Warrior: Sarah Winnemucca Hopkins's Campaign for American Indian Rights, 1864–1891*. Lincoln: University of Nebraska Press, 2015.

Stephens, Autumn. *Wild Women: Crusaders, Curmudgeons, and Completely Corsetless Ladies in the Otherwise Virtuous Victorian Era*. Berkeley, CA: Conari Press, 1992.

Stewart, Patricia. "Nevada's Paiute Princess." In *Nevada Official Bicentennial Book*, edited by Stanley W. Paher. Las Vegas: Nevada Publications, 1976.

———. "Sarah Winnemucca." *Nevada Historical Society Quarterly* 14, no. 4 (1971): 23 38.

Turner, Erin H. *Wise Women: From Pocahontas to Sarah Winnemucca, Remarkable Stories of Native American Trailblazers*. Guilford, CT: TwoDot, 2009.

Winter, Jonah. *Wild Women of the Wild West*. New York: Holiday House, 2011.

Zanjani, Sally. *Devils Will Reign: How Nevada Began*. Reno: University of Nevada Press, 2007.

———. *Sarah Winnemucca*. Lincoln: University of Nebraska Press, 2001.

3. Helen Jane Wiser Stewart

Cleere, Jan. *More Than Petticoats: Remarkable Nevada Women*. Guilford, CT: TwoDot, 2005.

Evans, K. J. "Helen Stewart." *Las Vegas Review-Journal*, February 7, 1999.

"Helen Jane Wiser Stewart." Women's Research Institute of Nevada. University of Nevada, Las Vegas, 2014. Accessed at http://wrinunlv.org.

Hopkins, A. D., and K. J. Evans, editors. "Helen J. Stewart." In *The First 100: Portraits of the Men and Women Who Shaped Las Vegas*, p. 15–18. Las Vegas: Huntington Press Publishing, 1999.

Laux, Kimber. "Story of LV Valley Female Pioneer Lives On." *Las Vegas Review-Journal*, August 27, 2017.

Miller, Linda Karen. *Early Las Vegas*. Charleston, SC: Arcadia Publishing, 2013.

Nevada State Museum. *The Letters of Helen J. Stewart*. Las Vegas: Nevada Museum Association, 2009.

"Pioneer Citizen of Las Vegas is Called by Death." Obituary: Helen J. Stewart. *Las Vegas Review-Journal*, March 12, 1926.

Porter, Carrie Townley. "Helen J. Stewart." Nevada Women's History Project. Accessed at http://www.unr.edu/nwhp.

Seagraves, Anne. *High-Spirited Women of the West.* Lakeport, CA: Wesanne Publications, 1992.

Townley, Carrie Miller. "Helen J. Stewart: First Lady of Las Vegas." *Nevada Historical Society Quarterly* 16, no. 1 (Spring 1974): 3–32.

Zanjani, Sally, and Carrie Townley Porter. *Helen J. Stewart: First Lady of Las Vegas.* Las Vegas: Stephens Press, 2011.

4. FELICE COHN

Abrams, Jeanne E. *Jewish Women Pioneering the Frontier Trail: A History in the American West.* New York: New York University Press, 2006.

Cleere, Jan. *More Than Petticoats: Remarkable Nevada Women.* Guilford, CT: TwoDot, 2005.

———. *Nevada's Remarkable Women: Daughters, Wives, Sisters, and Mothers Who Shaped History*, 2nd ed. Guilford, CT: TwoDot, 2015.

Cohn, Felice. "Women of Nevada Interested in Politics." In *Women of the West*, edited by Max Benheim. Los Angeles: Publisher's Press, 1928.

"Featured Historic Nevada Woman: Felice Cohn." *Nevada Women's History Project News* 11, no. 2 (May 2006): 8–10.

Felice Cohn Papers, 1884–1961. Nevada Historical Society, Reno, Nevada.

"Felice Cohn—A Woman of Action." *Nevada State Journal*, May 2, 1932.

Ford, Jean. "Felice Cohn." Nevada Women's History Project. Revised by Kay Sanders, 2008. Accessed at https://www.unr.edu/nwhp.

Ford, Jean, Janet White, and Janet Wright. "Cohn was Nevada's Youngest Lawyer Ever." *Reno Gazette-Journal*, March 26, 2008.

Gafford, Mary. "Felice Cohn." In *Skirts That Swept the Desert Floor*, edited by M. A. Duval. Las Vegas: Stephens Press, 2006.

Kogan, Lisa V. *With Strength and Splendor: Jewish Women as Agents of Change.* New York: Women's League for Conservative Judaism, 2008.

Marschall, John P. *Jews in Nevada: A History.* Reno: University of Nevada Press, 2008.

Moore, E. "Smith Valley Colony." In *Nevada Official Bicentennial Book*, edited by Stanley W. Paher. Las Vegas: Nevada Publications, 1976.

"Nevada's Only Woman Attorney Here on Business." *Goldfield Daily Tribune*, August 15, 1907.

"Obituary of Morris Cohn." *Nevada Appeal*, March 5, 2005.

Pollak, Oliver B. "Felice Cohn." In *Jewish Women: A Comprehensive Historical Encyclopedia*. Jewish Women's Archive, March 1, 2009. Accessed at https://jwa.org.

Rocha, Guy. "Myth #72: Stepping Up to the Bar: Female Attorneys in Nevada." *Sierra Sage*, Carson City/Carson Valley, Nevada, January 2002.

Rocha, Guy, and John Marschall. "Dispelling Myths of State's First Native Female Lawyer." *Reno Gazette-Journal* 18 (April 6, 2008).

"Today in 1879: Female Attorneys Are First Allowed to Practice before the Supreme Court." *Legal Solutions Blog*. February 15, 2013. Accessed at http://blog.legalsolutions.thomsonreuters.com.

Watson, Albert S. "Letter from Albert S. Watson to E. C. Brown." Goldfield Mining Company, October 16, 1905. Miscellaneous records. Bancroft Library, University of California, Berkeley.

Watson, Anita Ernst. *Into Their Own: Nevada Women Emerging into Public Life*. Reno: Nevada Humanities Committee, 2000.

"Woman's Protest Against Woman Suffrage." *Leslie's Weekly*, July 31, 1913.

"Women's Legal History." Bar Association, Stanford University, July 18, 1997. Accessed at http://wlh.law.stanford.edu.

5. Wuzzie Dick George

Dick, S. "US Indian Census, 1933–34." Walker River Agency, Nevada.

Ford, Victoria. "Wuzzie George." In *Skirts That Swept the Desert Floor*, edited by M. A. Duval. Las Vegas: Stephens Press, 2006.

Ford, Victoria. "Wuzzie Dick George." Nevada Women's History Project. Revised by Lois Kane, May 2010. Accessed at http://www.unr.edu/nwhp.

———. "Wuzzie George—Folk Artist Teacher, Tribal Elder." *Nevada Women's History Project News* 4, no. 4 (November 1999): 8–9.

Fowler, Catherine S. *Tule Technology: Northern Paiute Uses of Marsh Resources in Western Nevada*. Smithsonian Folklife Studies 6, 1990.

Nevada Historical Society Indian Baskets. Accessed at https://www.youtube.com/watch?v=ARoCa5R7rLQ.

Raven, Nancy. *Wuzzie Comes to Camp*. Bloomington, IN: Trafford Publishing, 2008.

"Stewart Indian School History." Nevada Indian Commission. Accessed at http://stewartindianschool.com/history/.

Thompson, Bonnie. *The Student Body: A History of the Stewart Indian School, 1890–1940*. PhD diss., Arizona State University, 2013.

"Tule Technology: Northern Paiute Uses of Marsh Resources in Western Nevada." Office of Folklife Programs, Smithsonian Institution. Film, 1981. Includes footage by Margaret Wheat.

Wheat, Margaret M. "Oral History Interview with Wuzzie George." Margaret M. Wheat Collection. Special Collections Department, University of Nevada, Reno. Accessed at http://contentdm.library.unr.edu.

———. *Survival Arts of the Primitive Paiutes*. Reno: University of Nevada Press, 1967.

6. Anna Frances Elleser Rechel

Boone, Donald. "Rawhide Scrapbook." *Desert Magazine* 26, no. 5 (May 1963): 10-11.

Carlson, Helen S. *Nevada Place Names: A Geographical Dictionary*. Reno: University of Nevada Press, 1974.

Ford, Victoria. "Anna Frances Elleser Rechel." Nevada Women's History Project. Accessed at http://www.unr.edu/nwhp.

———. "Anna Frances Elleser Rechel." In *Skirts That Swept the Desert Floor*, edited by M. A. Duval. Las Vegas: Stephens Press, 2006.

"Hawthorne Youth Is Taken by Death." *Nevada State Journal*, July 13, 1937. Also published in *Reno Gazette-Journal*, July 13, 1937.

Kille, J. Dee. "United by Gold and Glory: The Making of Mining Culture in Goldfield, Nevada, 1906–1908." PhD diss., University of Nevada, Reno, 2008.

Muir, John. "Nevada's Dead Towns." In *The Writings of John Muir: Steep Trails*. Boston/New York: Houghton Mifflin, 1918.

"Nevada Town Swept from Map by Cloudburst." *Colorado Springs Gazette*, September 1, 1909.

"Rawhide." Mineral County Museum. Accessed at http://web2.greatbasin. net/~mcmuseum/rawhide.htm.

"Rawhide Annie: A Rawhide Legend." High Desert Drifters. 2006. Accessed at http://www.highdesertdrifter.com.

"Rawhide Has Just 1 Resident." *The Indianapolis Star*, December 26, 1965.

"Rechel Thrived as a Prospector, but Never Struck It Rich." *Reno Gazette-Journal* 11 (March 1, 2010).

Shamberger, Hugh A. *The Story of Rawhide*. Carson City: Nevada Historical Press, 1970.

Weight, Harold O. "When Rawhide Roared." *Desert Magazine* 10, no. 8 (June 1947): 6–10.

Zanjani, Sally. *A Mine of Her Own, Women Prospectors in the American West, 1850–1950*. Lincoln: University of Nebraska Press, 1997.

7. Thérèse Alpetche Laxalt

Atxirika, Victoria Bañales. *Literary Portraits of Basque-American Women from Shadow to Presence*. PhD diss., University of the Basque Country, May 2015.

"Basque Country: Smithsonian Opens Doors to a Unique European Culture." *The Washington Post*, June 29, 2016.

"Basques." Countries and their Cultures. Accessed at http://www.everyculture.com.

Davies, Richard O., editor. *The Maverick Spirit: Building the New Nevada*. Reno: University of Nevada Press, 1999.

Douglass, William A. "The Basques of Nevada." In *Nevada Official Bicentennial Book*, edited by Stanley W. Paher. Las Vegas: Nevada Publications, 1976.

Douglass, William A., and Richard H. Lane. *Basque Sheep Herders of the American West: A Photographic Documentary*. Reno: University of Nevada Press, 1985.

Echeverria, Jeronima. *Home Away from Home: A History of Basque Boardinghouses*. Reno: University of Nevada Press, 1999.

Ford, Jean. "Therése Alpetche Laxalt." Nevada Women's History Project. Accessed at https://www.unr.edu/nwhp.

Haraway, Fran. "Therese Laxalt." In *Skirts That Swept the Desert Floor*, edited by M. A. Duval. Las Vegas: Stephens Press, 2006.

Hulse, James W. *The Silver State*, 2nd ed. Reno: University of Nevada Press, 1998.

Laxalt, Paul. Interview. *Nevada Magazine*, 2008.

———. *Nevada's Paul Laxalt: A Memoir*. Reno: Jack Bacon & Company, 2000.

Laxalt, Robert. *Sweet Promised Land*. New York: Harper & Row, 1957.

———. *Travels with My Royal: A Memoir of the Writing Life*. Reno: University of Nevada Press, 2001.

Lerude, Warren. *Robert Laxalt: The Story of a Storyteller*. Reno: University of Nevada Press, 2013.

"A Lifetime of Stories." *Reno Gazette-Journal* 19 (November 7, 1999).

Moreno, Richard. *A Short History of Carson City*. Reno: University of Nevada Press, 2011.

"Nevada's 'Mother of the Year.'" *Nevada State Journal* 18 (May 14, 1967).

Osa, Mateo. "Robert Laxalt Oral History." Sheepherders of Northern Nevada: A Multimedia Exhibit. Center for Basque Studies, University of Nevada, Reno. Accessed at https://knowledgecenter.unr.edu.

Pesek, Margo Bartlett. "Nevada Festivals Celebrate Basque Heritage." *Las Vegas Review-Journal*, June 7, 2015.

Turner, Frederick. *Of Chiles, Cacti, and Fighting Cocks: Notes on the American West*. New York: North Point Press, 1990.

Urza, Monique Laxalt. *The Deep Blue Memory*. Reno: University of Nevada Press, 1993.

8. MARY HILL FULSTONE

American Mothers Committee. *Mothers of Achievement in American History, 1776–1976: Bi-centennial Project, 1974–1976*. North Clarendon, VT: C. E. Tuttle Co., 1976.

Bunkowski, Terry. "Dr. Mary Hill Fulstone." Nevada Women's History Project. Accessed at https://www.unr.edu/nwhp.

Bunkowski, Terry, and Nancy Sansone. "Dr. Mary Hill Fulstone." In *Skirts That Swept the Desert Floor*, edited by M. A. Duval. Las Vegas: Stephens Press, 2006.

Centers for Disease Control and Prevention. "Estimated Influenza Illnesses, Medical Visits, Hospitalizations, and Deaths Averted by Vaccination in the United States." Accessed at https://www.cdc.gov.

"Dr. Mary Fulstone." *Yerington Mondays*, January 7, 2016. Accessed at http://yeringtonmondays.blogspot.com.

"Fulstone, Dr. Mary: Recollections of a Country Doctor in Smith, Nevada." Oral history conducted by M. E. Glass (1973–1974). Reno: University of Nevada Oral History Project, 1980.

"Fulstone Girls Win Twin Title National Crown." *Nevada State Journal* 12 (January 3, 1950).

Funk, A. W. "She's Nevada's Favorite Doctor." *Pacific Southwest Airlines Magazine*, November 1982.

Paher, Stanley W., editor. *Nevada Official Bicentennial Book*. Las Vegas: Nevada Publications, 1976.

Riley, B. "Smith Valley's 'Dr. Mary' Still Active at 83." *Nevada State Journal* 1 (November 23, 1975).

"Smith Valley Site of Fulstone Service." *Reno Gazette-Journal*, December 6, 1987.

US Congress. "Dr. Mary Fulstone." *Congressional Record.* 94th Congress, Second Session. 122, no. 53 (April 8, 1976).

Westergard, Dixie. *Dr. Mary: The Story of Mary Hill Fulstone, M.D., a Nevada Pioneer.* Reno: Jack Bacon & Company, 2004.

9. ALICE LUCRETIA SMITH AND BERTHA WOODARD

"Alice Lucretia Smith." *Nevada Women's History Project News* 5, no. 2 (May 2000): 7.

Alice L. Smith Papers. Special Collections. University of Nevada, Reno: 1938–1988.

Brean, Henry. "Divorce Capital: Six-week Split Spurred Nevada Economy." *Las Vegas Review-Journal,* January 19, 2014.

Brown, Matthew B. "Black History in Nevada." *Nevada Magazine*, January/February, 2014.

Corey, Michael. "African-Americans in Nevada." *Nevada Historical Society Quarterly* 35, no. 4 (Winter, 1992): 239–57.

Del Cohen, Shane, editor. *300+ Facts About the African-American Experience in Northern Nevada.* Reno: Our Story, Inc., 2016.

Fate, Michael. "Gulfside Assembly." BlackPast. Accessed at http://www.blackpast.org.

Harmon, Mella. "Reno and the African American Divorce Trade: Two Case Studies." *Online Nevada Encyclopedia*, January 3, 2011. Accessed at http://www.onlinenevada.org.

Harmon, Mella Rothwell. "Divorce and Economic Opportunity in Reno, Nevada during the Great Depression." Master's Thesis, University of Nevada, Reno, 1998.

"Klansman Parade in Full Regalia." *Nevada State Journal* 8 (October 18, 1924).

LeMere, Joan. "Alice Lucretia Smith." In *Steadfast Sisters of the Golden State*, edited by Joan Burkhart Whitely. Las Vegas: Stephens Press, 2013.

"NAACP Endorse Assembly Bill, Cite Lawmakers." *Reno Evening Gazette* 9 (February 10, 1960).

National Association for the Advancement of Colored People. Records, 1951–1965. Manuscript Collection. Special Collections Library, University of Nevada, Reno.

Nevada Historical Society Docent Council. *Early Reno*. Charleston, SC: Arcadia Publishing, 2011.

Nevada State Legislature. "Memorializing Distinguished Civil Rights Leader Bertha Woodard." Senate Concurrent Resolution No. 27. Accessed at https://www.leg.state.nv.us.

"Passion in the Desert." *Fortune Magazine* 9, no. 4 (April 1934): 100–107, 124–32.

"Reno Civil Rights Leader Bertha Woodard Dies." *Las Vegas Sun*, September 22, 1999.

Reno Divorce History. "Divorce in Popular Culture: The Silver Screen." Accessed at http://renodivorcehistory.org.

Reno-Sparks NAACP Branch No. 1112, Reno-Sparks NAACP Past-Presidents. Accessed at http://www.renosparksnaacp.org.

Rusco, Elmer R., project director. Nevada Black History Project. *Nevada Black History: Yesterday and Today*. Reno: Nevada Humanities Committee, 1992.

Sanders, Kay. "Alice Lucretia Smith." Nevada Women's History Project. Accessed at http://www.unr.edu/nwhp. Reprinted *Reno Gazette-Journal*, March 20, 2019.

Sansone, Nancy. "Bertha Rosanna Sanford Woodard." In *Steadfast Sisters of the Golden State*, edited by Joan Burkhart Whitely. Las Vegas: Stephens Press, 2013.

Swallow, C. F. "The Ku Klux Klan in Nevada during the 1920s." *Nevada Historical Society Quarterly* 24, no. 3 (Fall 1981): 203–20.

Smith, Alice. *Voices of Black America*. Reno: Bureau of Governmental Research, University of Nevada, 1971.

"Ulysses S. Woodard." *Nevada Evening Gazette*, March 28, 1973, editorial.

Westbrook, Juanita. "Alice L. R. Smith: Busier Than a Cranberry Merchant." *Nevada Humanities Chautauqua* 10 (June 25, 2014).

10. LILLY ONG HING FONG

Bokelmann, Dorothy. "Lilly Hing Fong." Nevada Women's History Project. 2008. Accessed at http://www.unr.edu/nwhp.

Bokelmann, Dorothy, and Jean Spiller. "Lilly Hing Fong." In *Steadfast Sisters of the Golden State*, edited by Joan Burkhart Whitely. Las Vegas: Stephens Press, 2013.

"California, Passenger and Crew Lists, 1882–1959." In *Passenger Lists of Vessels Arriving at San Pedro/Wilmington/Los Angeles, California*. The National Archives, Washington, DC.

Carter, Gregg Lee. "Social Demography of the Chinese in Nevada: 1870–1880." *Nevada Historical Society Quarterly* 28, no. 2 (1975).

Chase, Linda. *Picturing Las Vegas.* Layton, UT: Gibbs Smith, 2009.

Chinese Historical Society of America. *Remembering 1882: Fighting for Civil Rights in the Shadow of the Chinese Exclusion Act.* 2012. Accessed at http://www.civilrightssuite.org/1882/.

Chung, Sue Fawn, and the Nevada State Museum. *The Chinese in Nevada.* Charleston, SC: Arcadia Publishing, 2011.

Coulombe, Peggy. "ASU's First Recipient of the Warner-Fong Fellowship Announced." School of International Letters and Culture, Arizona State University. March 27, 2013. Accessed at https://silc.clas.asu.edu.

Foley, Kathleen, and others, editors. *50 Years of Nevada Spirit.* Nevada State Bank, 2009.

Fong Biographical File. Lied Library. Special Collections, University of Nevada, Las Vegas.

Fong Elementary School. "Our Namesake." Accessed at http://fongeswebsite.wixsite.com.

"Fongs' Garden." A menu. University of Nevada, Las Vegas University Libraries. Accessed at http://d.library.unlv.edu/digital/collection/menus/id/5133/rec/2.

Goodall, Lois. "Interview with Kenneth W. Fong." Oral History Research Center, University of Nevada, February 22, 2014.

Hawley, Tom. "Video Vault: Fong's Garden Family Influential in Las Vegas." *KSNV News,* July 22, 2015.

Hogan, Jan. "Wing and Lilly Fong Left Mark on Las Vegas through Education, Philanthropy." *Las Vegas Review-Journal,* September 6, 2011.

Hopkins, A. D., and K. J. Evans, editors. "Wing and Lilly Fong." In *The First 100: Portraits of the Men and Women Who Shaped Las Vegas.* p. 15–18. Las Vegas: Huntington Press Publishing, 1999.

James, Ronald. "Chinese in Nineteenth-Century Nevada." *Online Nevada Encyclopedia,* January 11, 2011. Accessed at http://www.onlinenevada.org.

Koch, Ed, and Eric Leake. "Las Vegas Businessman, Banker, Developer Fong Dies at 79." *Las Vegas Sun,* May 25, 2005.

Moor, Angela. "Lilly Fong." *Online Nevada Encyclopedia,* January 29, 2008. Accessed at http://www.onlinenevada.org.

"Services Set for Former Regent Fong." *Las Vegas Sun,* March 21, 2002.

Shum, Annie Yuk-Siu. "An Interview with Lilly Fong: An Oral History." Ralph Roske Oral History Project on Early Las Vegas. University of Nevada, February 29, 1980.

Simich, Jerry L., and Thomas C. Wright, editors. *The Peoples of Las Vegas: One City, Many Faces*. Reno: University of Nevada Press, 2005.

Takaki, Ronald. *Strangers from a Different Shore*. Boston, MA: Little, Brown and Company, 1998.

Willis, Stacy J. "Journeys on Charleston." Nevada Public Radio, July 25, 2016.

Woodbury, Stacy. *All For God, Home, and Country: A History of the First One Hundred Years of the Daughters of the American Revolution in Nevada*. Morgan Hill, CA: Bookstand Publishing, 2009.

11. Velma Bronn Johnston

Cruise, David, and Alison Griffiths. *Wild Horse Annie and the Last of the Mustangs: The Life of Velma Johnston*. New York: Scribner, 2010.

Denver Public Library. Archives of Correspondence: Velma B. Johnston Special Collection, Denver, Colorado.

Downer, Craig C. "Velma Bronn Johnston a.k.a. 'Wild Horse Annie.'" Nevada Women's History Project. Accessed at https://www.unr.edu/nwhp.

Haraway, Fran. "Velma Bronn Johnston." In *Steadfast Sisters of the Golden State*, edited by Joan Burkhart Whitely. Las Vegas: Stephens Press, 2013.

Henry, Marguerite. *Mustang: Wild Spirit of the West*. Chicago: Rand McNally, 1966.

International Society for the Protection of Mustangs and Burros. "The Story of Wild Horse Annie." Accessed at http://www.ispmb.org.

Kania, Alan J. *Wild Horse Annie: Velma Johnston and Her Fight to Save the Mustang*. Reno: University of Nevada Press, 2012.

Reid, Harry. "Joint Resolution Recognizing Wild Horses as National Heritage." SJ 149 IS, 101st Congress, 1989.

Ryden, Hope. *America's Last Wild Horses*. New York: Ballantine, 1970.

Scranta, Corky. *The Wild Ones: The Legacy of Wild Horse Annie*. Alpharetta, GA: BookLogix, 2015.

Walter, Harold. "Wild Horses West." *Sierra Magazine*, July 1959, 10–14.

"The Wild Horse Annie Act." American Wild Horse Campaign. Accessed at https://americanwildhorsecampaign.org/wild-horse-annie-act.

12. Sarann Knight Preddy

Bracey, Earnest N. "The Moulin Rouge Mystique: Blacks and Equal Rights in Las Vegas." *Nevada Historical Society Quarterly* 39, no. 4 (Winter 1996): 272–88.

Chase, Linda. *Picturing Las Vegas.* Layton, UT: Gibbs Smith, 2009.

Cook, Kevin. "The Vegas Hotspot That Broke All the Rules." *Smithsonian Magazine*, January 2013. Accessed at http://www.smithsonianmag.com.

Fink, Jerry. "Not Forgotten." *Las Vegas Sun*, October 22, 2000.

"Former Owner of Moulin Rouge Preddy Dies." *Las Vegas Sun*, July 15, 1999.

Goodrich, James R. "Negroes Can't Win in Las Vegas." *Ebony Magazine* 1 (March 1954).

Goodwin, Joanne, and Claytee White. "Sarann Knight Preddy, Entrepreneur." *Online Nevada Encyclopedia*, January 3, 2011. Accessed at http://www.onlinenevada.org.

Hershwitzky, Patricia. *West Las Vegas*. Charleston, SC: Arcadia Publishing, 2011.

"History of Henderson." *Las Vegas Sun*, April 16, 2003.

Lucky Coin Productions. "The Gaming Queen," YouTube Video, April, 2012. Accessed at https://www.youtube.com/watch?v=JV3LNm34rFI.

Munks, Jamie. "County Gets Moulin Rouge Site." *Las Vegas Review-Journal*, October 20, 2017.

Philpot, Parker. "Sarann Knight Preddy: Las Vegas Early Gaming Pioneer Remembered." *Las Vegas Tribune*, December 25, 2014.

Preddy, Sarann Knight. *72 Years in Las Vegas*. Las Vegas: PBQ Printing, 2015.

Rusco, Elmer R. "The Civil Rights Movement in Hawthorne, Nevada." *Nevada Historical Society Quarterly* 43, no. 1 (Spring 2000): 35–73.

"Sarah Ann Knight Preddy." Ninth episode in *Makers—Women in Nevada History*. Vegas Public Broadcasting Service, 2015. Accessed at https://www.youtube.com/watch?v=DFYFu7f2JVM.

"Sarann Knight Preddy: Activist Puts Her Mark on Nevada." *Las Vegas Black Image Magazine*, August 9, 2010.

Simich, Jerry L., and Thomas C. Wright, editors. *The Peoples of Las Vegas: One City, Many Faces*. Reno: University of Nevada Press, 2005.

Taloma, Cassandra. "Gaming Pioneer, Civil Rights Icon Knight Preddy dies." *Las Vegas Review-Journal*, December 22, 2014.

White, Claytee D. "An Interview with Sarann Preddy." Las Vegas: Vegas Women in Gaming and Entertainment Oral History Project, 1998.

13. Geneva Ann Smith Douglas

Bliss, Laura. "Atomic Tests Were a Tourist Draw in 1950s Las Vegas." The Atlantic City Lab. August 8, 2014. Accessed at http://www.citylab.com.

Boy Scouts of America. "Merit Badges: Nuclear Science." Accessed at http://www.scouting.org.

Douglas, Geneva S. *A Community Monitoring Program Surrounding the Nevada Test Site: One Year of Experience.* Washington, DC: US Department of Energy, 1983.

Federal Radiological Monitoring and Assessment Center (FRMAC): The First 25 Years. Washington, DC: National Nuclear Security Administration, 2010.

Friends of Nevada Wilderness. Accessed at http://www.nevadawilderness.org.

Geneva Douglas Papers. Nevada Women's Archives. Special Collections, number 93-35, University of Nevada, Reno.

"Geneva Smith Douglas '54, Radiation Scientist." Obituaries. *Colby Magazine* 82, no. 3 (April 30, 1993): 70.

Gragg, Larry. *Bright Light City: Las Vegas in Popular Culture, 1905–2005.* Lawrence, KS: University Press of Kansas, 2013.

Haber, Heinz. *The Walt Disney Story of Our Friend the Atom.* New York: Simon & Schuster, 1956.

"Let's Get a Fair Shake for Nevada." *Reno Gazette-Journal*, August 16, 1988.

Martin, Gary. "D.C. Gets Yucca Firestorm: Regulatory Agency to Open Comment Period, but Ire Flowing Early." *Las Vegas Review-Journal*, May 31, 2017.

PBS. *Las Vegas: An Unconventional History.* Film Transcript, 2012. Accessed at http://www.pbs.org.

Powers, Ashley. "Tourists Revisit the Cold War at Nevada Test Site." *Los Angeles Times,* July 17, 2011.

"Radiological Emergency Response Plan, United States Federal." *Encyclopedia of Espionage, Intelligence, and Security.* Accessed at http://encyclopedia.com.

"Report Says Nuclear Tests Sent Radioactive Debris over L.A. Area in 1950s." *Battle Creek Enquirer*, March 11, 1979.

Rothman, Hal K. *The Making of Modern Nevada.* Reno: University of Nevada Press, 2010.

Scanlan, Laura Wolff. "Nuclear Nevada." National Endowment for the Humanities, July 31, 2011. Accessed at https://www.neh.gov.

Schrag, Philip G. "Seeing Ground Zero in Nevada." *The New York Times*, March 12, 1989.

"Smith, Edna L." Obituary. *Gloucester Daily Times*, June 8, 1983.

Titus, A. Costandina. *Bombs in the Backyard: Atomic Testing and American Politics*. Reno: University of Nevada Press, 2001.

———. "Cultural Fallout in the Atomic Age." In *History and Humanities: Essays in Honor of Wilbur S. Shepperson*, edited by Francis X. Hartigan, p. 121–36. Reno: University of Nevada Press, 1998.

Watson, A. E. *Into Their Own: Nevada Women Emerging into Public Life*. Reno: Nevada Humanities Committee, 2000.

Wilkins, S. "Geneva Smith Douglas." Nevada Women's History Project. Accessed at http://www.unr.edu/nwhp.

———. "Geneva Smith Douglas." In *Skirts That Swept the Desert Floor*, edited by M. A. Duval. Las Vegas: Stephens Press, 2006.

Women's Research Institute of Nevada. "Geneva Smith Douglas." March 16, 2011. Accessed at http://wrinunlv.org.

14. MARCIA DE BRAGA

Barker, Larry. "Silver State Rodeo Back in Fallon." *Nevada Appeal News Service*, July 1, 2008.

Bosshart, Becky. "Sarah Winnemucca Statue to be Unveiled in DC." *Nevada Appeal*, March 7, 2005.

"Childhood Leukemia Clusters in Fallon, NV." In *Field Hearing before the Committee on Environment and Public Works, United States Senate, One Hundred Seventh Congress, First Session on Responses by the Federal Government to Disease Clusters Resulting from Possible Environmental Hazards*. Washington, DC: US Government Printing Office, April 12, 2001.

Clanton, Carol. "Marcia de Braga." Nevada Women's History Project, November 2010. Accessed at https://www.unr.edu/nwhp.

Corkill, Bunny, and Keith Weaver. "Marcia Smith Murdock de Braga." In *Churchill County: In Focus*. Fallon, NV: The Churchill County Museum Association, 2009–2010.

"de Braga, Marcia." Obituary. *Reno Gazette-Journal*, March 26, 2010.

de Braga, Marcia. *Dig No Graves: A History of Churchill County*. Sparks, NV: Western Printing and Publishing Company, 1964.

"Fallon Parents Celebrate Bottled-Water Victory." Associated Press, December 9, 2003. Accessed at http://www.kolotv.com.

Gorman, Tom. "Nevada Town's Residents Unperturbed about Arsenic in Its Drinking Water." *Los Angeles Times*, April 9, 2001.

Haraway, Fran. "Marcia Smith de Braga." In *Steadfast Sisters of the Golden State*, edited by Joan Burkhart Whitely. Las Vegas: Stephens Press, 2013.

Lerner, Steve. *Sacrifice Zones: The Front Lines of Toxic Chemical Exposure in the United States*. Cambridge, MA: MIT Press, 2010.

Miller, Geralda. "Paiute Teacher, Lecturer, Scout, Interpreter & Civil Rights Worker Split by Ideologies in Life, Nevadans Now Share Hall." *Reno Gazette-Journal*, March 9, 2005.

Ranson, Steve. "Marcia de Braga's Efforts Centered on Her Love for People." *Nevada Ranch & Farm Exchange* 9 (Summer 2010).

"Remembering a Miracle Worker in Nevada." *Reno Gazette-Journal*, April 4, 2010.

Seney, Donald B. "Marcia de Braga." Bureau of Reclamation's Newlands Project Oral History Series. Denver, CO: Bureau of Reclamation, 2008.

"Welcome to Fallon: Description, History" Accessed at http://www.nv-landmarks.com/towns-fg/fallon.htm.

"What Caused Small Town's Leukemia?" Associated Press, December 15, 2003.

Zanjani, Sally S. *Devils Will Reign: How Nevada Began*. Reno: University of Nevada Press, 2006.

INDEX

Kay Moore was born and raised in Maryland, where she was surrounded by many sites of historical significance. Exploring these turned her into an incorrigible history buff with a special interest in the lives of women and children. Upon retirement from California State University, Sacramento, Kay moved to Las Vegas, where she and her grandchildren now explore the historical sites of Nevada. She is the author of several nonfiction young adult books, including *Bold Women in California History* and the award-winning *The Great Bicycle Experiment: The Army's Historic Black Bicycle Corps, 1896–97.*

Written for ages 12 and up, the Bold Women series features women who pushed through adversity to carve their own paths and achieve their personal dreams. Their stories prove what women can accomplish when they dare to be BOLD.

Other Books Available in this Series

Bold Women in Alaska History

Bold Women in California History

Bold Women in Colorado History

Bold Women in Indiana History

Bold Women in Michigan History

Bold Women in Montana History

Bold Women in Texas History

MP Mountain Press
PUBLISHING COMPANY
P.O. Box 2399 • Missoula, MT 59806 • 406-728-1900
800-234-5308 • info@mtnpress.com
www.mountain-press.com